WITHDRAWN

Activities
in the
Earth Sciences

by Helen Challand, Ph.D.

illustrations by Len Meents

CHILDRENS PRESS ™

CHICAGO

Library of Congress Cataloging in Publishing Data

Challand, Helen J.
  Activities in earth sciences.

  (Science activities)
  Includes index.
  Summary: Activities and experiments—such as
making charcoal, measuring shadows, and
calculating the speed of sound—in the areas
of astronomy, weather, and geology.
  1. Astronomy—Experiments—Juvenile
literature. 2. Weather—Experiments—Juvenile
literature. 3. Geology—Experiments—Juvenile
literature. [1. Earth sciences—Experiments.
2. Experiments] I. Meents, Len W., ill.
II. Title. III. Series.
QB46.C44 1982   550′.7′8   82-9444
ISBN 0-516-00506-5   AACR2

    8 9 10 11 12 R 90 89

TABLE OF CONTENTS

CHAPTER 1
Geology

CHAPTER 2
Astronomy

CHAPTER 3
Weather

Chapter 1
Geology

MAKING SOIL

Soil is a combination of broken rock and dead organic material. Collect a variety of rocks, mainly sedimentary rocks such as sandstone and limestone. Rub one rock against another, collecting the particles in a jar. Rocks also

may be put in a cloth bag and hammered until they are pulverized. How long does it take to make a cup of soil? Add bits of dead leaves, grasses, and animal remains. What forces in nature over thousands of years have produced the soil on the ground today? Can you see a need for the conservation of this natural resource? It takes from several hundred to a thousand years to make one inch of soil.

For additional information see page 81

DEFINITIONS

natural resources — all the land, water, energy, mineral wealth, and naturally occurring plants and animals in any region.

organic — pertaining to, derived from, or composed of living organisms.

pulverized — crushed or ground into small particles.

sedimentary — formed by or pertaining to sediment; sedimentary rocks were formed from compressed minerals or organic sediments and pieces of earlier rocks.

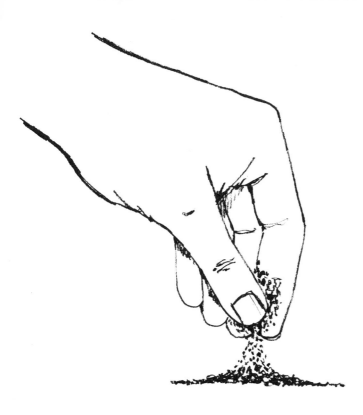

CLASSIFYING SOILS BY TOUCH

To determine soil texture, moisten a sample and rub it between your fingers. Identify the sample by comparing the way it feels to the list of classes below.

1. Sand — a mixture, but largely sand; coarse and gritty to the touch; separate particles are easily seen; doesn't hold together when moist, but falls apart in your hands as separate grains.

2. Sandy loam — holds together when moist, but hardly makes a smear on your fingers.

3. Silt loam — makes some smear when moist, but when rubbed doesn't thin out like clay before becoming rough and broken.

4. Clay loam —makes smears midway between silt loam and clay when moist; easily crushed between fingers when dry; particles are difficult to distinguish.

5. Clay — a mixture, but largely clay; sticky and plastic when wet, and difficult to crush when dry; when moist and rubbed between fingers, makes a smooth thin continuous smear; separate particles can be seen only under a microscope.

DEFINITIONS

loam — a fertile soil composed of varying amounts of silt, clay, sand, and humus.

SORTING SOIL WITH SIEVES

Soil sieves are commercial devices sold at science supply houses. They are a group of cylinders with wire mesh bottoms. The cylinders stack on top of each other. The wire mesh for the pans has different-size holes. The largest holes are in the top tray, and the smallest holes in the bottom tray.

Dig up a six-inch cube of soil from an area to be analyzed. Spread it out on newspaper until it is thoroughly dry. Use a rolling pin or jar to roll out lumps as fine as possible. Pick out twigs and rotting leaves. These can be added to the top cylinder, which collects the humus.

Pour the crushed soil into the top pan, put on the lid, and shake until particles fall through the sieves. There are usually six pans labeled from top to bottom: humus, coarse gravel, fine gravel, coarse sand, fine sand, silt, and clay. The latter is the finest of soil particles.

Using a measuring cup or similar container, pour the samples from each pan into the cup and record amounts. Figure out the percentage of each type in the soil sample. Good soil usually has around equal parts of humus, sand, silt, and clay. The combination is called loam.

DEFINITIONS

analyze — to study the separate parts of which a thing is composed.

humus — the dark-brown organic substance found in soil formed by decay of organic matter, a natural fertilizer.

silt — a sediment of earth or mineral particles smaller than particles of sand; commonly carried by streams and rivers and deposited at the river mouth; may form a delta.

Number each seive:

3. fine gravel

4. coarse sand
5. fine sand
6. silt
7. clay

2. coarse gravel   1. humus

EXTRACTING THE SOIL HORIZONS

A profile of the soil in any location normally will display three layers. The topsoil or Horizon A is the richest. It is composed of loam and decaying vegetation or humus. Horizon B or the subsoil usually is lighter in color, and often is more compacted with a higher content of clay. Horizon C is a layer of sand and rocks minus any humus. It rests on bedrock, the parent material of a region. For example, in the middle western United States the parent rock is limestone, since much of the area was once the floor of the Silurian Sea.

To secure a profile of soil it is best to use a commercial soil borer. However, you can get a rough profile by using a narrow spade. Dig a small hole at a slight angle so you can lift up a spadeful without disturbing it. Lay it carefully onto a newspaper. Dig deeper in the same hole and attempt to get a second

COLLECTING SOILS

Fill clear plastic containers or glass jars with samples of sand, silt, clay, and loam. It would be interesting to add to the collection samples of soils from various parts of the country, gathered during a vacation trip. Make labels for the containers, noting classification and location information about each sample.

Soils are made up of three kinds of particle groups, or separates. These separates are sand, silt, and clay. No soil found in nature consists of only one of these separates. It is always a combination. These combinations are called classes.

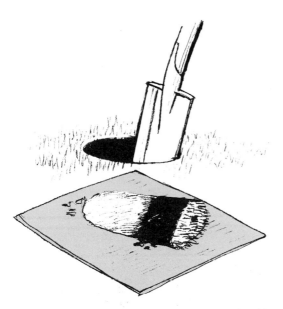

spadeful lower down. Lay this in line with the first. Can you distinguish the horizons? Measure each layer. Take samples from other places—woods, open fields, vacant lots. Record the land contours of the sites. Does this make a difference in the amount of topsoil?

DEFINITIONS

bedrock — solid, massive rock, usually covered by soil or broken pieces of rock.

contour — external outline or shape; the boundary of a figure.

decay — the slow process of breaking down dead things.

extracting — drawing forth.

humus — the dark-brown organic substance found in soil formed by decay of organic matter, a natural fertilizer.

loam — a fertile rich soil composed of varying amounts of silt, clay, sand, and humus.

site — the place, scene, or point of something.

CONSERVING TOPSOIL

Use three plastic pie pans. Cut a hole near the top rim on one side of each pan. Tape a piece of plastic tubing to each hole. Put layers of clay, loam, and sand mixture in each pan. Add a top layer of rich topsoil. Rest one end of each pan on a block of wood to elevate it at a thirty-degree angle. Direct the free end of each tube into a dish.

In one pan make rows across the pan and plant a cereal grain—wheat, oats, or barley. In the second pan make rows in the opposite direction, up and down, and plant the same crop. Do not plant anything in the third pan.

When the seedlings are about two inches tall, use a sprinkling can to pour the same amount of water (rain) over each pan. What happens to the topsoil in each case? Measure the amount of soil that collects in the dishes. Do you see how topsoil can be conserved?

For additional information see page 81

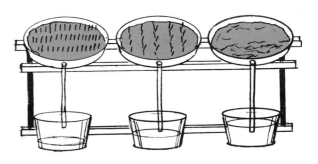

13

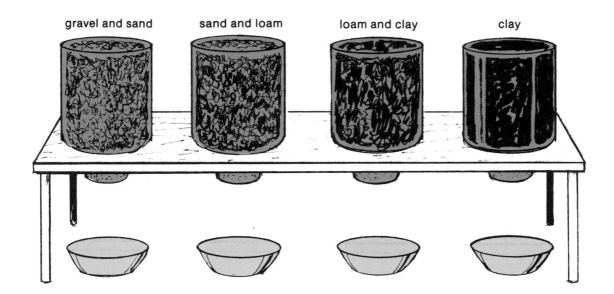

gravel and sand   sand and loam   loam and clay   clay

DETERMINING WATER RETENTION OF SOILS

Use four clear plastic bottles. Saw off the bottom of each bottle. Build a small plywood stand to hold the bottles upside down. Tape a piece of gauze over the mouth of each bottle. Fill one with gravel and sand, the second one with sand and loam, the third with loam and clay, the fourth with clay. With a spoon, press all the different types of soil firmly into the jars. Place dishes under each to catch the drippings.

With a partner helping, at the same time pour a cup of water into the top of each bottle. Observe the length of time it takes water to pass through each type of soil. Which type lets the water run right through? Which is the slowest? Which would you select if you were gardening or farming?

For additional information see page 81

DETERMINING FACTORS NECESSARY FOR HUMUS BREAKDOWN

Fill four clay pots with good topsoil from a garden or woods. Place the first pot in an oven and heat it to 400°F for half an hour. Cut four one-inch cubes of raw potato. Bury a cube in each pot two inches below the surface of the soil. The second pot should never be watered. Put the third pot in the refrigerator and the fourth pot in a sunny window. Do not disturb your experiment for two weeks. At the end of that time carefully remove the soil from each potato. What happened to each piece? Which one decayed the most? What two groups of plants, the decomposers in a food chain, live in soil releasing the minerals in the humus? What conditions are the best for these soil organisms?

DEFINITIONS

decay — the slow process of breaking down dead things.

decompose — to break down into simpler substances.

food chain — the interrelationship, in a green community, between the plants, the plant-eating animals (herbivores), the animal-eating animals (carnivores), and the animal or plant-eating animals (omnivores).

humus — the dark-brown organic substance found in soil formed by decay of organic matter, a natural fertilizer.

mineral — a natural occurring, inorganic substance with a definite chemical composition, characteristic crystalline structure, and distinctive chemical properties.

organism — a plant or animal.

SHOWING THE FORMATION OF ESKERS, KAMES, AND MORAINES

In many parts of the United States the landforms were made by glaciers that moved down from the north and then slowly melted. To understand how these were created, make a model of a glacier.

Locate a sandbox or put a couple of pails of sand in a large container. Wet the sand well in order to mold a rough depression in the shape of a half-moon and about two to three inches deep. The sides should slope. Push several rocks and small pebbles around on the floor of the depression. Build up a small snakelike ridge about an inch high from the back to the leading edge of the depression. This will form an esker, which is a raised riverbed from a river that once flowed under the glacier.

To produce a kame, make a cone-shaped piece out of cardboard. Push the point of the cone into the sand on the bottom so that it stands upright.

Mix a batch of plaster of paris to the consistency of thin pudding. Carefully pour this into the depression, over the rocks and around the inverted cone. You may need to make several batches to fill the depression if you are making a glacier at least a foot wide and long. Before the plaster sets, press some pebbles into the top and sprinkle sand over it. Scoop out a trough of plaster from the back edge to the cardboard cone. This illustrates a river on top of a glacier. Place a few small rocks around the front rim of the cone. As the flowing river met this obstruction it whirled, grinding a hole in the glacier and forming a kame. A kame is a hill of sorted rocks and sand with the finest particles at the top, made by the sorting action of a stream.

When huge chunks of ice broke off from the main body of the glacier and then melted, they formed potholes, ponds, and small lakes. Make small plaster models of these to show how an area can be pockmarked with water holes. From your state geology department secure a map of the county in which you live. It will be marked with landforms that should help you to understand what your area looked like thousands of years ago.

When your homemade glacier is hard, it can be picked up. It is ready to be used to demonstrate its effect on an area of land. Smooth out a bed of sand and set the glacier into it. Push it down and forward. The smooth surface will be marked with eskers, kames, and moraines at the leading edge of the glacier.

FINDING OUT ABOUT BUOYANCY

Weigh a rock with a spring scale. Put the rock in a jar of water with the spring scale still attached. How much does the rock weigh now? What is the buoyant force on the rock? Experiment with a variety of rocks of different sizes and weights. Can you arrive at a ratio and state the principle first proposed by a Greek scientist named Archimedes?

For additional information see page 82

DEFINITIONS

esker — a long narrow ridge or mound of sand, gravel, and boulders deposited by a stream flowing on, within, or beneath a stagnant glacier.

glacier — a large body of ice moving slowly down a slope or valley or spreading outward on a land surface.

kame — a short ridge, hill, or mound of stratified drift deposited by glacial meltwater.

DEFINITIONS

buoyant — the power of a liquid to exert an upward force on a body placed in it.

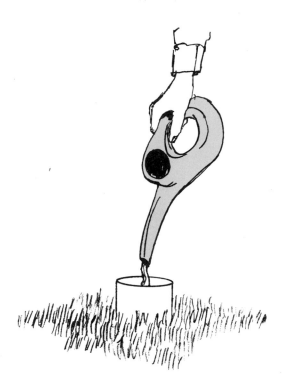

It would be helpful to use a soil borer in each location to get a profile of the soil texture below the surface. What happens to compacted soil during a rainstorm? What type of soil is best for plant growth and other organisms in the soil?

For additional information see page 82

DEFINITIONS

organism — a plant or animal.

porous — having very fine holes through which substances, such as water or air, can pass.

MEASURING THE POROSITY OF SOILS

Remove the tops and bottoms from several identical cans. Select a day when it has not rained for at least a week. Find three different locations for this test: a grassy spot (lawn), bare soil (path or ball diamond), and a low or high place (ravine or hill).

Drive a can halfway into the soil by pounding on a piece of wood placed on top of the can. Put a halfway mark on the outside of the can so you will know when it is driven in the correct distance. Pour water into the can to the rim. Record the time it takes for the water to percolate or soak into the soil in each of the three locations. Can you explain the results? Which soil was the most porous?

MEASURING THE SLOPE OF A HILL

With a partner to help, use two yardsticks and a level to measure the slope of a hill. Place one end of a yardstick against the ground on a slope, raising the lower end (which is pointing downhill) until the yardstick is level. Place the second yardstick perpendicular to the first against the 33-1/3-inch mark on it. Move the second stick down until it touches the ground. Read the number of inches on it where it meets the first one. This figure multiplied by three will give you the percent of the slope.

Another method is to use a clinometer. Glue a plastic protractor to one end of a heavy strip of cardboard (1″ X 10″). Hammer a small nail or a tack part way into the cardboard and through the center of the baseline of the protractor. Tie a six-inch thread to this nail with a small nail tied to the free end of the thread. When this device is held parallel to the ground the thread should bisect the ninety-degree mark on the protractor.

Now take the clinometer outside and find a hill or slope to try it on. Stand on the slope facing uphill. Hold the cardboard at eye level so that you can sight up its length to the top of the hill. With your free hand trap the thread against the protractor until you can read the number of degrees that the thread was on. This gives the angle of the slope. Figuring the angle of a slope is helpful in farming and in the construction of buildings and roads.

DEFINITIONS

clinometer — a small surveying instrument held in the hand to measure vertical angles; can also be used as a level.

parallel — equally distant at all places.

perpendicular — standing upright at right angles to plane of the horizon.

protractor — a device shaped in a half circle with 180 degrees marked on it; used to measure angles.

1 inch = 2.5 centimeters

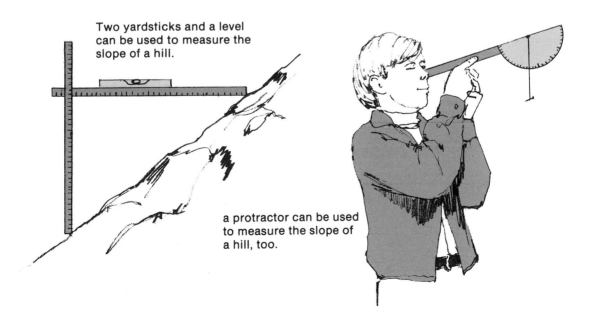

Two yardsticks and a level can be used to measure the slope of a hill.

a protractor can be used to measure the slope of a hill, too.

CLASSIFYING ROCKS

The first test to perform is to rate the hardness of a mineral. Geologists use a standard table (Mohs Hardness Scale) to classify the hardness of rocks. The scale from soft to hard is this: 1 - talc, 2 - gypsum, 3 - calcite, 4 - fluorite, 5 - apatite, 6 - feldspar, 7 - quartz, 8 - topaz, 9 - corundum, and 10 - diamond.

Any rock that can be scratched with a fingernail has a hardness of 1 or 2 on the scale. Minerals that can be scratched with a penny are 3 on the hardness scale. A knife will scratch those with a hardness of 4 or 5. Minerals on the scale at 6 and 7 will scratch glass. Number 8 on the scale will scratch quartz and 9 will scratch topaz. A diamond, number 10, is used in a glass cutter and will scratch all the other rocks plus another diamond.

The acid test is very simple. Rocks containing calcite or lime will bubble or fizz when an acid is poured on them. Use vinegar as the acid. If you hold the rock close to your ear and listen carefully, you'll be able to hear the fizzing.

The third test is cleavage. When you break rocks, they will either cleave (an easy, flat break) or fracture, depending on the minerals present in them. Some cleavages are good clues to identifying minerals in rocks. The way a rock fractures is also a clue to its identity. Hit a rock with a hammer to break it. Place a cloth over the rock before you hit it so that chips won't fly. Use the cleavage chart for help in identification.

A fourth method for identification is called the streak test. When you scratch a piece of unglazed white porcelain (the back of a bathroom tile) with certain rocks, they make characteristic streaks. For example, although pyrite in rock form looks yellow, it always leaves a black streak on tile. Identify your specimens by using the adjoining chart.

To group your rocks according to whether they are igneous, sedimentary, or metamorphic, use the following general descriptions of the three kinds of rocks. Compare your samples with the classification pictures. Sedimentary rocks have a layered appearance, but usually break easily and feel gritty. Igneous rocks have a crystalline appearance, with the crystals mixed and never in layers. Metamorphic rocks are very hard and more crystalline than igneous rocks, but the crystals of each mineral are lined up in bands or layers.

For additional information see the chart on page 88

DEFINITIONS

acid — any of a group of chemical compounds that taste sour, turn blue litmus red, and can neutralize bases.

cleave — the way an object splits.

geologist — a person who studies the structure, composition, and history of earth.

igneous — pertaining to any rock formed by the melting action of heat followed by slow or rapid cooling of a magma, with or without crystallization.

metamorphic — describes a rock that has been changed by tremendous pressures and heat which lines up the crystals in layers.

mineral — a natural occurring, inorganic substance with a definite chemical composition, characteristic crystalline structure, and distinctive chemical properties.

sedimentary — formed by or pertaining to sediment; sedimentary rocks were formed from compressed minerals or organic sediments and pieces of earlier rocks.

CAUTION: THIS ACTIVITY MUST BE DONE WITH AN ADULT PRESENT.

MAKING CHARCOAL

This activity should be done under the supervision of an older person. Puncture a hole in the lid of a coffee can. Place several small sticks (½" x 3") of hardwood in the can. Replace the lid. Heat the can over a Bunsen burner or hot plate to drive out the water vapor in the wood. As wood gas escapes from the hole, light a match to it until all the gas is burned up. Remove the can from the heat and allow it to cool. What is the color of the end product?

Try to collect rocks about the same size. Don't try to carry big boulders. Select rocks about the size of chicken eggs. You will need two of each kind —one for your permanent collection and one to run tests on for identification purposes. Use masking tape to number each sample and record the location where it was found. Wrap your samples in newspaper before depositing them in the canvas bag. Some rocks are soft and this protects them from crumbling while they are carried back home for classification.

DEFINITIONS

quarry — a large hole in the ground left when slate or stone has been removed or excavated.

COLLECTING ROCKS

Rock samples can be found almost everywhere. Take along a canvas bag, hammer, chisel, and goggles. Never hammer a rock unless you are wearing protective goggles and are at least ten feet away from other people. Look for specimens along roadways and railroad tracks, in vacant lots and quarries. Get permission to collect on private property.

MAKING A PLANKTON DIP NET

The many kinds and numbers of tiny to microscopic plant and animal life in bodies of water are called plankton. Taking a sample from a stream, marsh, bog, swamp, river, lake, or an ocean gives a reading on the healthiness of the aquatic habitat.

Cut off the foot of a nylon stocking. Fasten this end to the neck of a small bottle with a string or strong rubber

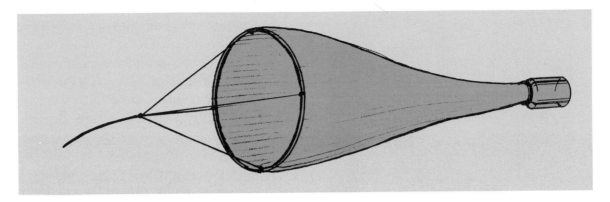

band. Sew the other end to a cylinder of heavy wire. Tie four six-inch pieces of cord to the wire and tie these cords to a single long line.

Standing on the bank of a river or lake, hang on to the end of the line while throwing the bottle and net out into the water as far as the length of the line will allow. Avoid hitting any rocks unless the bottle is plastic. Carefully drag in the net. Small life in the water will be trapped in the bottle as the water goes through the net.

You will end up with a concentrated solution of organisms. Using the naked eye, a magnifying glass, and a microscope, diagram all plants and animals in detail for identification later. Since there are so many in such a small amount of water they soon will die from lack of oxygen. There are books available to help identify those algae and protozoa that thrive in polluted waters or only in clean waters. If you do a rough population count while examining drop after drop of plankton, you can figure out if the body of water is in a stage of being polluted.

Plankton nets can be used to capture microscopic plant and animal life in water.

DEFINITIONS

algae — any of the simplest green plants, ranging in size from one-celled diatoms to huge kelp.

aquatic — growing in or living in water.

concentrate — containing a relatively high proportion of solute to solvent, said of a solution.

habitat — the natural environment of a particular animal or plant; marshy land is the habitat of ducks.

microscopic — too small to be seen by the eye alone; refers usually to objects at least 150 millimicrons in diameter (within range of regular optical microscope).

organism — a plant or animal.

plankton — small plant and animal organisms in water that drift with currents and have little locomotive ability of their own, especially those at or near the surface.

protozoa — a phylum of one-celled animals which are represented in almost every kind of habitat, and some of which are serious parasites of man and other animals.

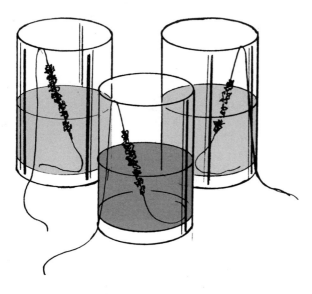

GROWING CRYSTALS

Experiment with growing crystals from a variety of solutions. Use half a glass of boiling water for each kind. Mix as much powdered alum in the hot water as it will hold. Tie a weight to the end of a string. Drop the weight in the glass of alum solution with the other end of the string hanging over the side. Let the solution cool slowly. Observe the diamond-shaped crystals clinging to the string. Also try using borax, Epsom salts, copper sulfate, and sodium hyposulfite. Can you see the differences in the kinds of crystals?

Now try this, using one of the chemicals, such as the salt. You have the one which was cooled to room temperature. Set up two more salt solutions. Place one in the refrigerator and the other in a freezer overnight. Remove and compare the size of the crystals that were cooled at varying rates. At which temperature did the largest crystals form?

Break up brick or charcoal into small pieces. Place several pieces in the center of a bowl. Mix one-fourth cup of salt, one-fourth cup of liquid bluing, one-fourth cup of water, and one tablespoon of ammonia.

Pour the solution over the pieces of coal or brick. Fill a medicine dropper with food coloring and drop small amounts over the pieces. Set the dish aside now while the crystals grow. The crystals will crumble easily so don't move the dish.

Watch and note when the first crystals appear and how fast they develop. Crystals are formed because water is drawn into the brick or coal, leaving solids behind. The ammonia, bluing, and salt form a complex crystal. Use a hand lens to observe the shape.

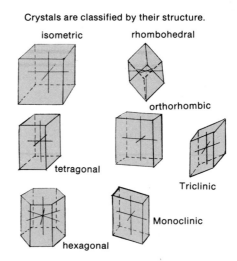

Crystals are classified by their structure.

isometric

rhombohedral

orthorhombic

tetragonal

Triclinic

Monoclinic

hexagonal

DISCOVERING HOW FOSSILS WERE MADE

Fossils usually are found in three forms: the actual plant or animal, the petrified specimen, or an imprint. While traveling, you may be able to visit petrified forests or find an actual shell or bone of an animal in rock. At home, you can make an imprint such as might have been made by a dinosaur.

Prepare a mixture of equal parts of cement, sand, and lime. Add water until it is about the consistency of thick pudding. This mixture is similar to sandstone, a sedimentary rock that contains many fossils. Pour the mixture into a shallow box. Just before it sets, press a shell, a leaf, or an animal's foot into the surface of the mixture. Permit the mixture to harden without disturbing it.

Another way to make fossils is with clay and plaster of paris. Push modeling clay into a shallow box. Smooth the surface. Press parts of organic objects, such as leaves or shells, into the clay and remove them. Mix plaster of paris and water to the consistency of thick soup. Pour this over the clay and let it set. Remove the box and clay from the plaster mold. A negative fossil impression is left on the plaster. Grease the top of this impression and pour a second layer of plaster over it. When the mixture sets, the two pieces can be separated. The top mold is then the positive print.

DEFINITIONS

fossil — any trace of plant or animal life of a previous geological age found in the earth's crust, such as impressions, organic parts, and wholly or partially petrified material.

organic — pertaining to, derived from, or composed of living organisms.

petrified — having the bodily remains of organisms change partly or completely to stone by the exchange of minerals from those dissolved in water.

sedimentary — sedimentary rocks were formed from compressed minerals or organic sediments and pieces of earlier rocks.

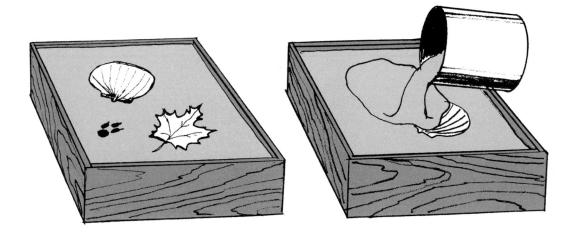

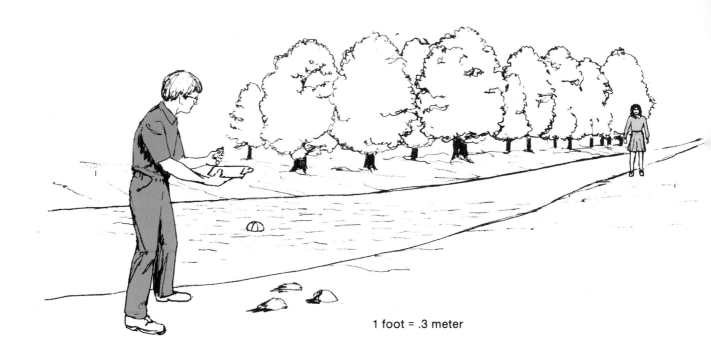

1 foot = .3 meter

CALCULATING THE FLOW SPEED OF STREAMS AND RIVERS

Two people are needed for this activity. Mark off a 100-foot distance along the bank of a stream or river. One person should stand at each marker. The distance can be greater if you still are able to see or hear each other. The one at the starting point tosses an object—a rubber ball, piece of wood that floats, or a wad of aluminum foil—into the middle of the flowing stream. Be sure it is clear of shoreline plants. At the second the object hits the water, start the stopwatch. The partner downstream should wave an arm or yell out the second the object is directly in front of him or her. Immediately click off the stopwatch.

Record the minutes and seconds. With a paper, pencil, and a little math skill you can calculate the flow speed into miles per hour, knowing that there are 5,280 feet in a mile.

WEATHERING ROCKS

What effects do heat and cold have on rocks? Place different kinds of small rocks on a hot plate for ten minutes or longer. With a pair of tongs pick up the rocks, one at a time, and place them in a pan of ice water. Observe what happens.

Which types of rocks (sedimentary, metamorphic, or igneous) react the most to temperature changes?

Locate a piece of sandstone, limestone, or other sedimentary rock. Measure and record its exact size. Tie a length of cord around it in four directions. Find a fast-moving stream or river in which to put the rock. Fasten the other end of the cord to an object along the bank. After several weeks retrieve the rock and remeasure it. What has the water done to it?

Find a rock covered with lichen. Dampen a strip of blue litmus paper and lay it next to where the plant is attached to the rock. Does it change color? What does this tell you about the effect of growing plants on rocks? Scrape away the lichen from the rock and notice that particles of the minerals are crumbling away. Lichens, a symbiotic relationship of algae and fungi, are called the pioneers of soil building. Can you see why? What other plant could live on bare rock and start the process of weathering?

DEFINITIONS

algae — any of the simplest green plants.

fungi — plants that lack chlorophyl.

igneous — pertaining to any rock formed by the melting action of heat followed by slow or rapid cooling of a magma, with or without crystallization.

lichen — an alga and a fungus growing together in symbiotic association on a solid surface.

litmus paper — a product made from the purple coloring found in certain lichens; used as an acid base indicator, It turns red in acid and blue in base.

metamorphic — describes rock that has been changed by tremendous pressures and heat which lines up the crystals in layers.

sedimentary — sedimentary rocks were formed from compressed minerals or organic sediments and pieces of earlier rocks.

symbiotic — the intimate living together of two dissimilar organisms in a relationship.

For additional information see page 82

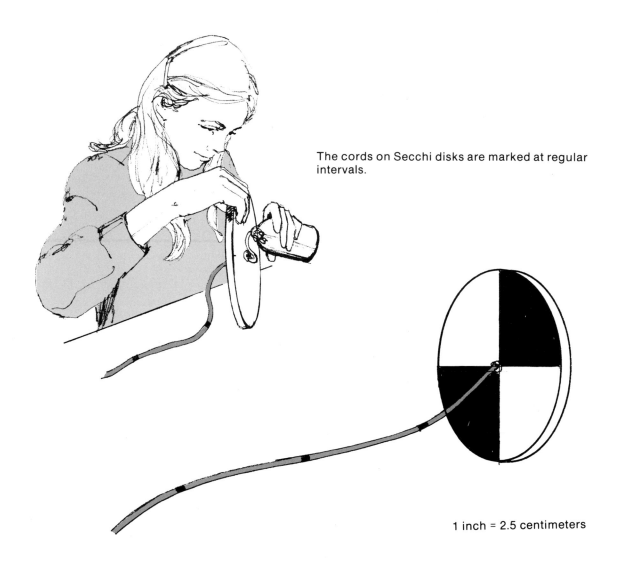

The cords on Secchi disks are marked at regular intervals.

1 inch = 2.5 centimeters

DESIGNING A SECCHI DISK

A Secchi disk is a device used by limnologists and naturalists to determine the cloudiness of a body of water. As pollutants are dumped into streams and lakes, clear water becomes murky. How many lakes can you stand in up to your neck in water and see your feet on the bottom?

Cut a circle of wood about nine inches in diameter. Draw lines similar to those cutting a pie into four pieces. Paint alternate pieces black and white. Drill a hole in the center of the disk and push through a heavy cord. Tie a weight on the underside and a knot above to hold the disk on the end of the line. For ease in figuring measurements while using the Secchi disk, mark off six-inch intervals on the cord with black paint.

To determine the cloudiness of a body of water it is best to take a reading away from the shallow shoreline. From a bridge over a stream or river, lower the disk. Count the six-inch marks as you lower the disk in the water. When you can no longer see the black and white disk, record the final distance. The transparency of water in a lake can be determined at the end of a pier or during boating expeditions.

DEFINITIONS

diameter — the length of a straight line through the center of an object.

limnologist — a person who studies freshwater lakes and ponds including physical and geographical features and classification, and flora and fauna.

naturalist — a person involved in the study of life in nature.

transparency — refers to a material that light can pass through.

SETTING UP A BERLESE FUNNEL

Good soil has a variety of living as well as dead organisms in it. You will need a widemouthed jar, large funnel, small piece of wire screen, and a lamp. Set up the apparatus by following the adjoining illustration.

To check the soil in a particular area use a spade to dig up the amount of soil the funnel will hold. Place it in the funnel and leave the lamp on overnight. The heat from the lamp, plus the soil drying out at the surface, will cause the living organisms to burrow deeper into the funnel, finally dropping through the wire screen into the jar.

The insects, worms, larvae, arachnids, and tiny crustaceans can be identified and a population count can be made. Collect samples from different locations and run this test. Is there life in a sandy beach? To find out, put a piece of gauze over the screen in the funnel.

DEFINITIONS

arachnid — the class of animals in phylum arthropoda, including spiders, scorpions, mites, ticks, and daddy longlegs; arachnids have four pairs of jointed legs, no wings, and no antennae.

crustacean — a class of largely aquatic arthropods with segmented bodies covered by a hard substance called chitin, and numerous segmented appendages; vary from microscopic organisms to the twelve-foot-wide giant crab; included among crustaceans are crayfish, lobsters, shrimps, crabs, barnacles, and various water fleas such as daphnia.

larva — an early form of an animal that undergoes a change in its development; in four stage metamorphosis, the larva is the form hatched from the egg; a caterpillar is the larva of a moth or butterfly while a tadpole is the larva of a frog.

organism — a plant or animal.

Be sure the light is shining directly down on the soil in the funnel.

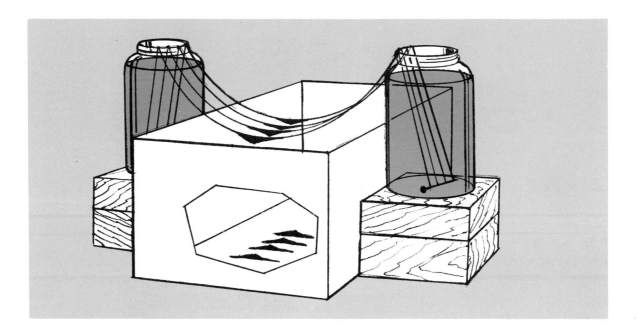

MAKING STALACTITES AND STALAGMITES

Construct a mock-up of an underground cavern with a cardboard or metal box. Follow the illustration or pattern the project after one you have seen. Place two tall jars on either side of the box. Tie four or five pieces of heavy string to two nails. Make a supersaturated solution of Epsom salts and water. A little vegetable dye may be added for color. Fill the jars with the solution.

Place a nail in each jar with the strings leading over the top of the open box. Set the jars up on some object so that the center of each hanging string in the "cave" is below the level of water in the jars. Water and salt will move up the cord. As the water evaporates, the salt will accumulate. Let this alone for a week.

Soon piles of salt build up on the floor of your homemade cave. What are they called? The formations hanging from the strings (or cave roof) are referred to as what?

For additional information see page 82

DEFINITIONS

evaporate — to change from liquid to gas; to remove a liquid, such as water from a substance, often by heating.

supersaturated — dissolving a chemical in a liquid until no more will dissolve at a given temperature.

31

DEMONSTRATING
WAVE EROSION

Fill one end of a large dishpan with sand, sloping it down to the center. Pour water in the other end until the pan is half full. Use an egg beater or your hand to create waves of water that move into the sand. Or lift up the water end of the pan an inch off the table and then set it down quickly to get waves moving into and away from the sand. What happens to the sandy shoreline? Create rough waves as if in a furious storm. Can you see how sand dunes are formed like those at the lower end of Lake Michigan? Stick some little plants along the shoreline. Repeat the wave acton. Can rough waters uproot the "trees"?

EXPERIMENTING WITH
CONVECTION IN WATER

This experiment will give one the idea of how the water in a lake "turns over." The bottom of a deep body of water is cold, while the surface area is heated by the sun.

Fill a glass container about half full of very hot water. Permit it to stand for a few minutes. Add very cold water slowly so that it forms a cool bottom layer. Put a few drops of laundry bluing or ink into the water. Notice how the color moves when it reaches the zone where the layers of water mix.

Place a few ice cubes in the water. Put drops of color on the cubes and watch the resulting flow. If possible, run some hot colored water in at the bottom of the container and watch its action. Examine the water closely with a bright light to view any small particles of lint or dust that might be moving about.

TESTING WATER

Water test kits are available from science supply houses. Simple kits furnish chemicals and directions for determining three factors: amount of dissolved oxygen, percentage of carbon dioxide, and the pH. More complex kits provide materials to calculate hardness and the presence of minerals.

When studying life in ponds, bogs, lakes, rivers, and oceans, it is helpful to test the water. A healthy water habitat for most plants and animals should have a reading of 8 ppm or more of dissolved oxygen. When the D.O. reading gets around 3 or 4 you will find little life in the water. A rippling, fast-moving stream usually will have a higher D.O. than a stagnant marsh has. Of course the amount of plant life in the water, releasing oxygen by photosynthesis, will affect the percentage.

The amount of carbon dioxide depends upon the degree of decomposition or decay. Life still thrives in streams that have 30 to 40 ppm of CO_2.

The pH of water is affected by the rock at the bottom of a body of water, the pollutants dumped into it, and the amount of decay. A reading of 7 (neutral) is best for most life. When it drops to 3 most living things are killed. Swimming in water with a pH reading of 3 would be almost as bad as swimming in vinegar.

DEFINITIONS

decay — the slow process by which a biological substance decomposes, generally by action of oxidizing bacteria or molds.

habitat — the natural environment of a particular animal or plant; marshy land is the habitat of ducks.

pH — a symbol indicating the acidity or basicity of a substance; a neutral substance neither acid nor basic, such as pure water, has a pH of 7.0.

photosynthesis — the production, by green plants, of simple sugar from carbon dioxide and water, releasing oxygen and water; occurs in chloroplasts of green plant cells and in the presence of light.

pollutant — something that pollutes or contaminates the environment. Bacteria, industrial waste, human waste, radioactive material, etc; can be pollutants.

stagnant — not moving; without current; a stagnant pool of water is often foul and odorous from lack of movement.

CREATING
A DELTA

Nail three boards (1″ X 4″ X 24″) together to form a long trough. Nail a square of wood on one end to close it off. Line the inside with foil or plastic to waterproof it. Fill the trough half full with rocks, small pebbles, sand, silt, and clay. This simulates the bottom of a stream or river. Set the open end of the trough on one end of a large cake pan and prop the closed end up at a slight angle so the water will run down to "the ocean" (cake pan).

Using a watering can, slowly pour a stream of water at the "head" of the river. As the water flows over the bottom it will carry particles with it to the "mouth" of the river. What happens as the water fans out in the cake pan? Which particles are deposited first? Last? Can you get a delta to form from the sediments the river is carrying?

For additional information see page 82

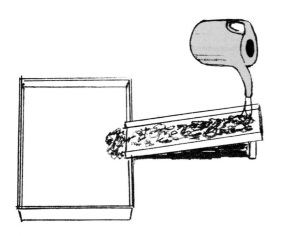

DEFINITIONS

delta — anything roughly triangular in shape, especially the alluvial deposit of soil or gravel by a large stream at the point of entry into the sea, usually resulting in numerous channels between the sea and main stream.

sediment — the matter that settles to the bottom of a liquid.

MEASURING EARTH'S
MAGNETIC FIELD

You can build an instrument that will show the influence of the earth's magnetic field. It is magnetism that causes the needle of the instrument to dip. The needle would be horizontal to the earth at the equator and would point straight down toward the earth at either of the magnetic poles.

Push a steel knitting needle all the way through a large cork so that the protruding ends are equal in length. It should be pushed through the large end of the cork, as close to the top as possible. Push a sewing needle into each side of the cork so the two are opposite each other. Balance the sewing needles on two water glasses so the knitting needle balances horizontally. Fasten a protractor to a block of wood so the top of it is level with the knitting needle. Put

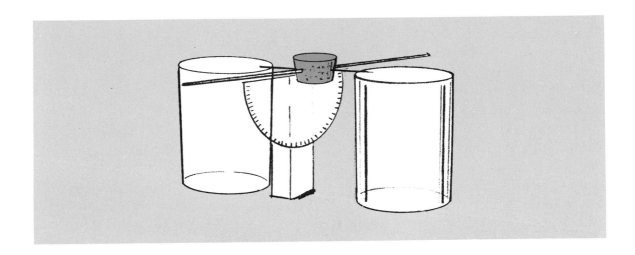

it between the glasses. If the knitting needle is turned downward, its point falls on the protractor scale.

Remove the cork and needles from the glasses. Find north with a compass. Point the sharp end of the knitting needle toward the earth's magnetic north pole. Hold two magnets with the north poles together so they form one strong magnet. Stroke one end of the knitting needle in one direction along the north pole of the double magnet. Hang the cork back on the glasses, so the needle points east and west. If the needle swings at all, both ends should dip equally. Immediately turn it so that the end of the needle which you have stroked with the north pole of the magnet points north (use the compass to make sure of this). If the needle swings, the north end should dip more sharply. The amount it dips depends on the strength of the magnets used and the length of time it was stroked. This does not indicate latitude. The purpose of the protractor is to help determine whether or not the needle is dipping at all. If you have trouble seeing this, a toothpick stuck in the bottom of the cork might help to see the dip.

DEFINITIONS

equator — the great circle of the celestial sphere whose plane is perpendicular to the axis of the earth.

latitude — the angular distance of any point north or south of the equator, measured in degrees from the equator, at 0 degrees.

magnetic field — the space near any magnet, which has lines of magnetic force through it; electric currents also generate magnetic fields.

protractor — a device shaped in a half circle with 180 degrees marked on it; used to measure angles.

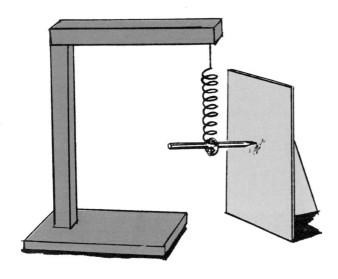

blunt object. What happens to the pen? Can you produce an image of vibrations or waves on the cardboard? A real seismograph employs a revolving cylinder which picks up the primary and secondary waves of an earthquake. When these devices are set up in a number of sites, observers are able to locate the position, extent, and strength of a quake.

RECORDING VIBRATIONS IN THE EARTH

Scientists use an instrument called a seismograph to record the pattern of waves when an earthquake occurs. A mock-up of this device can be made in the following way.

Purchase a spring from a hardware store. A section from a Slinky toy also would work. Or take a rather stiff wire and wind it around a pencil to form a short spring. Attach it to the crossbar of a wooden support. Mold a ball of Play Dough or clay on the end of the spring. Stick the top of a ball-point pen into the clay ball so that the pen is parallel to the surface of the table. Prop up a piece of white cardboard in front so the point of the pen just touches the cardboard.

Now you need to create an earthquake in the table, which represents the earth. Hit it hard with your fist or a

---

DEFINITIONS

seismograph — a sensitive device for recording and measuring vibrations at or below the earth's surface; used especially for detecting earthquakes and underground nuclear explosions.

Note: A seismograph is an instrument that records movement in the earth according to the Richter scale. The scale is from 1 to 9 and indicates the strength of an earthquake. Each number on the scale means the earthquake was 10 times stronger than the lesser number.

For example, earthquakes measuring 5 or less are considered minor because very little damage is done. But an earthquake measuring 7 is very serious. Many people can be killed and much property damaged. According to the richter measurement, the earthquake measuring 7 is twenty times stronger than the one measuring 5. An earthquake measuring 6 is ten times stronger than one measuring 5 on the scale.

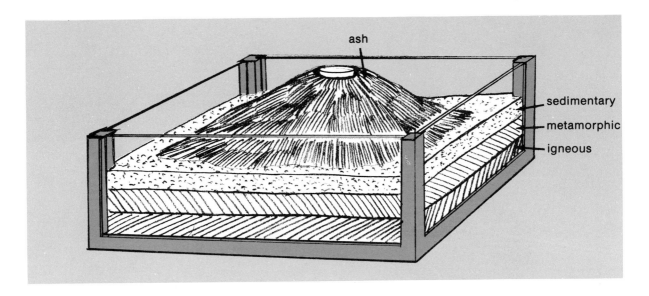

ash

sedimentary

metamorphic

igneous

DEMONSTRATING AN ERUPTING VOLCANO

Purchase several packages of different-colored modeling clay Let each color represent a kind of rock. The lower layer will be igneous, the second layer will be metamorphic, the top layer will be sedimentary. Construct a wood and glass frame for the cutaway of a volcano. Groove the wooden ends and base in order to slip in the glass sides. Leave one side open until the layers are modeled. Follow the illustration for details. Slip on the other glass side when completed.

Build up a volcanic cone on top, leaving a hole or crater. Insert a small metal can in the crater. Combine one teaspoon of fine ammonium dichromate crystals (from a drugstore or science supply house) and several match heads. Put this in the can. It burns when ignited, forming a dark green ash which tumbles over the cone in the same man-ner that lava flows from a real volcano, gradually building up into a mountain. CAUTION: Do not get any of the ash on your skin. It is an irritating chemical.

DEFINITIONS

igneous — pertaining to any rock formed by the melting action of heat followed by slow or rapid cooling of a magma, with or without crystallization.

metamorphic — describes a rock that has been changed by tremendous pressures and heat which lines up the crystals in layers.

sedimentary — sedimentary rocks were formed from compressed minerals or organic sediments and pieces of earlier rocks.

volcano — the cone-shaped mound built up on the surface of the earth when molten rock (magma) is forced up through an opening in the surface when heat is built up.

Chapter 2
Astronomy

MEASURING THE
SIZE OF THE MOON

Before tackling the job of figuring the width of the moon, begin with an object which enables you to verify your calculations. Hold a quarter out in front of your eyes until it just covers a round

object in the room, such as a clock face. Pretend you can't reach the clock face to measure it directly. You can determine the distance to it. Use this equation to figure the diameter of the clock.

$$\frac{\text{Diameter of clock}}{\text{Distance to clock}} = \frac{\text{Diameter of quarter}}{\text{Distance to eye}}$$

If you can work out that problem, go on to this one. Use the hole in a Life Saver to figure the moon's diameter. Pick a clear night when the moon is full. Check your calendar for the date. The distance to the moon is known, so you won't have to pace it out. The moon is about 240,000 (384,000 kilometers) miles away. Use the formula above. Check an encyclopedia to see how close you came to the correct distance.

SHOWING THE PHASES OF THE MOON

Set a lamp without a shade on a table in a dark room. Stand several feet away from the lamp. Hold a ball out in front of you so it is in line with your eyes and the bulb of the lamp. The light is the sun, the ball is the moon, and you are on the earth. Now move the moon (ball) slightly to the left of the bulb. How much of the moon is lighted at this point? Turn on your heels so that the ball moves in a circle. At which point is there a full moon? A new moon? A quarter moon?

Now work with the real moon. Every three nights for one month diagram the shape of the moon that is reflecting light. Date your pictures. If a night is overcast, leave a space in your series of drawings. Can you fill in the empty spaces at the end of the month to show the phases of the moon that did occur on those cloudy nights? Does the moon rotate as well as revolve?

For additional information see page 83

DEFINITIONS

diagram — a graphic design that explains rather than represents.

revolve — moving around another object.

rotate — turn on its axis; the earth's rotation produces day and night.

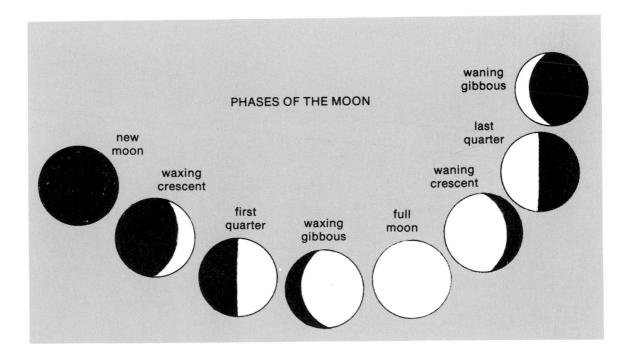

PHASES OF THE MOON

new moon

waxing crescent

first quarter

waxing gibbous

full moon

waning crescent

last quarter

waning gibbous

BUILDING PLANET MODELS

In order to see the relationship of the size of planets and their relative distance from the sun, construct models to scale. The accompanying chart provides the diameter of the planets and the number of inches each model should be made when one inch equals approximately four thousand miles. Models made of papier-mâché can be used. Shape each planet to the desired size and bake it in an oven for one-half hour. For each of the larger planets blow up a balloon to one inch less than the desired size. Mold a half-inch of papier-mâché over the balloon and let it dry for several days.

The planets can be suspended by strings from the ceiling of a room. Arrange them in order from the sun by

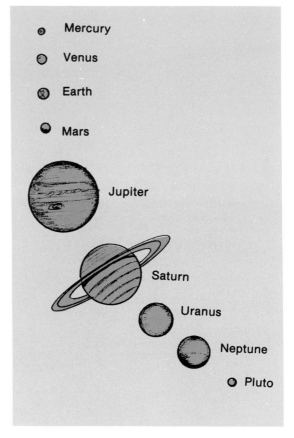

PLANET	MILES FROM SUN (Distance)	SCALE *1 (In inches)	DIAMETER IN MILES (Size)	SCALE *2 (In inches)
MERCURY	36,000,000	1.80	2,900	.75
VENUS	67,200,000	3.35	7,700	1.95
EARTH	92,900,000	4.65	7,920	2.00
MARS	141,500,000	7.10	4,215	1.05
JUPITER	483,300,000	24.15	85,700	21.45
SATURN	886,100,000	44.30	71,500	17.90
URANUS	1,783,000,000	89.15	32,000	8.00
NEPTUNE	2,793,000,000	139.65	27,700	6.95
PLUTO	3,670,000,000	183.50	3,600	.90

*1 one inch = 20 million miles
*2 one inch = 4,000 miles

PLANET	KILOMETERS FROM SUN	SCALE **1 (In centimeters)	DIAMETER IN KILOMETERS	SCALE **2 (In centimeters)
MERCURY	57,900,000	5.79	4,667	4.667
VENUS	108,150,000	10.815	12,392	12.392
EARTH	149,500,000	14.95	12,746	12.746
MARS	227,700,000	22.77	6,783	6.783
JUPITER	777,800,000	77.78	137,921	137.921
SATURN	1,426,000,000	142.6	115,068	115.068
URANUS	2,869,500,000	286.95	51,499	51.499
NEPTUNE	4,494,900,000	449.49	44,579	44.579
PLUTO	5,906,300,000	590.63	5,794	5.794

**1 one centimeter = 10,000,000 kilometers
**2 one centimeter = 1,000 kilometers

1 mile = 1.6 kilometers

following the chart. Moons and other bodies may be added to make your solar system more complete.

FINDING OUT ABOUT CENTRIFUGAL FORCE

Fill a pail one-third full of water. Swing it quickly up over your head and down in a circular fashion. The water clings to the bottom of the pail and does not spill out.

Put an inch of water in a round vase. Turn it rapidly sideways. Describe the position of the water in the vase. What is the relation of centrifugal force to the revolving object?

Fasten a one-pound weight to the end of a strong string. Holding the other end of the string, start swinging the weight in a circle. Swing it as fast as possible. Feel the pull on your arm. Replace the small weight with a heavier one. Repeat the circular motion. Is the pull on your arm greater? Were you able to increase centrifugal force?

For additional information see page 83

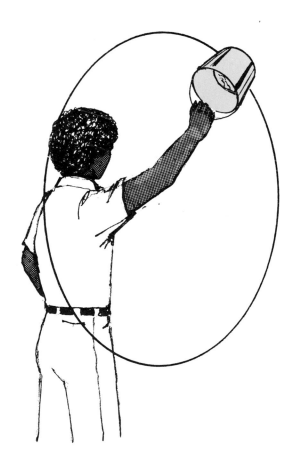

EXPERIMENTING
WITH GRAVITY

For this experiment you will need a stopwatch and a person who can throw accurately. Throw a ball ten feet (about one story) into the air. At the point where the ball stops and begins to descend, start the stopwatch. The instant the ball hits the ground stop the watch and record the time. Repeat the experiment throwing the ball about twice as high (twenty feet up) and again thirty feet up. Does the ball fall faster the higher it is thrown? A more accurate timing can be figured out if your partner drops a ball out of a first-, second-, and

third-story window of a building.

Line up several different coins along the length of a yardstick. Hold the yardstick over your head and tip it so that all coins fall off at the same time. Did you guess that the heavier coins would reach the ground first? What does happen? Do you know why?

Try dropping a Ping-Pong ball and a golf ball simultaneously from a second-floor window. Time the fall with a stopwatch. Be sure no one is underneath when you drop the balls. How long did it take each to reach the ground?

For additional information see page 83

MAKING A SUNDIAL

Cut the dial face out of a square of heavy wood. Cut a wooden triangle with a six-inch base to serve as the gnomon. The angle up the triangle depends on the latitude of your city. For example, Minneapolis is in the 45° latitude, so that should be the angle there. In Miami the angle would have to be 26°. Nail the gnomon on the dial face with the high point on the outside rim. Paint the dial with weatherproof paint. Anchor the sundial to a stake driven in the ground in a permanent place in an open area. Use a compass to line the gnomon with the North Pole.

When the sun's rays are directly overhead (no shadow on the dial face), mark the number "12" at this point. Continue to mark the numbers as each hour passes. The hour of 6:00 A.M. will be west of the low end of the gnomon, while 6:00 P.M. will be east. There will be some differences in tellng time on the dial and on your watch. There are only four days of the year when they match up: September 1, December 24, April 15, and June 15. These would be the best days to set up your sundial.

DEFINITIONS

gnomon — the pointer or similar vertical part of a sundial, whose shadow indicates the time.

latitude — an angular distance north or south from the earth's equator measured through 90 degrees.

SEPARATING SUNSHINE

Lean a pocket mirror in a glass of water. Set the glass on a table in front of a sunny window. As a beam of sunlight hits the water and mirror, some of the light rays are bent more than others. Direct light rays to a white wall or ceiling. The spectrum will range in a particular order. Can you find the order of these colors: indigo, red, green, violet, yellow, blue, and orange?

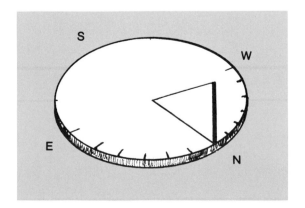

DEFINITIONS

spectrum — the colored bands of light produced by passing white or other complex light through a prism or diffraction grating, progressing from the longest wave length (red) to the shortest (violet).

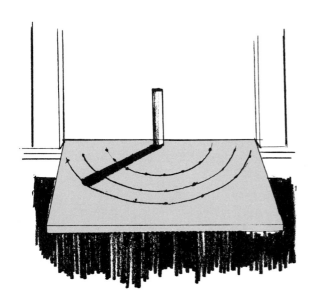

1 inch = 2.5 centimeters

MEASURING SHADOWS

Cut a piece of plywood (about 15″ X 20″). Erect a four-inch stick in the center of a longer side, about one inch from the edge. Place the board in a south window with the stick toward the south and the long sides running east and west.

At each hour of the day, make a dot at the end of the shadow and record the time. At night, connect the dots with a curved line. Repeat this monthly to record different curves as the sun reaches higher or lower angles. How does the length of the shadows change with the seasons? Does the average temperature go up or down as the sun moves higher in the sky and more directly overhead?

For additional information see page 83

DEMONSTRATING ECLIPSES

You will need a light source, two Styrofoam balls (one must be about four times larger than the other), and two sticks. Sharpen one end of each stick in order to push one into each of the balls. Hold the sticks so that the small ball (moon) and the large ball (earth) are in line with the light (sun). You will need to vary the distances each one is held from the sun and from each other. Start moving the moon counterclockwise in a orbit around the earth. At what point is a shadow thrown upon the moon? If you are standing on the earth, where would the moon have to be in relation to you and the sun to have a lunar eclipse? Move the moon in its orbit until part of the sun's rays are blocked. This is a solar eclipse. Why don't we have an eclipse every time there is a new or full moon? What is the pattern of our orbiting moon?

For additional information see page 83

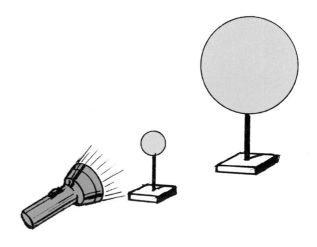

and set in the west? Continue to experiment and figure out why some places have longer days or night than others do.

How long are the days and nights in your area? Secure data from the daily newspaper. Record the figures for sunset and sunrise over a period of several weeks or longer. Use a bar graph, black for night and white for day, to display the changes.

EXPLAINING DAY AND NIGHT

Have a partner stand several feet away from you with a flashlight (sun). Hold a globe (earth) with the axis pointing at 23° in the northerly direction. Be sure the light of the flashlight strikes the globe. Which continents are on the lighted side? Which countries are having night? Now slowly turn the globe counterclockwise. Watch the circle of light fall on other places while those on the opposite side are moving into the dark side away from the sun. Do you see why the sun appears to rise in the east

45

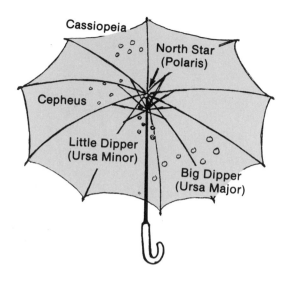

Cassiopeia
North Star (Polaris)
Cepheus
Little Dipper (Ursa Minor)
Big Dipper (Ursa Major)

LOCATING THE CONSTELLATIONS

Secure a star map from a science journal or newspaper Such a map is usually published monthly throughout the year.

Begin with the five constellations which appear to move around Polaris (the North Star). Secure a dark plain umbrella which can be drawn on with chalk. Draw the North Star around the very center of the unbrella, at the top of the handle. The North Star is at the end of the handle on the Little Dipper. Follow the commercial star map, filling in the positions of the stars in the Little Dipper, Big Dipper, Cepheus, Draco, and Cassiopeia. Use lines to connect the stars for each constellation. You are ready to go out on a clear night and study the sky.

Face north and locate Polaris and the rest of the Little Dipper. Hold the umbrella out in front of you and a little below your view of the five constellations. Turn the umbrella until it matches the patterns in the sky. You may need a flashlight to light up the umbrella if the moon is not full.

DEFINITIONS

constellation — any of nearly 100 arbitrary groupings of stars into real or fancied shapes: convenient for locating and identifying stars and other celestial objects.

Polaris — the bright star seen in the Northern Hemisphere that is almost directly above the earth's northern axis, also called the North Star.

EXPLAINING THE SEASONS

Take a globe and flashlight into a dark room. Put the light in a fixed position. Place the globe with the North Pole pointing straight up. Focus the light's strongest beam at the earth's equator. Now tilt the globe to an angle of about 23° so that the North Pole is nearest to the sun. What season is it in the Northern Hemisphere? The 23.5° inclination of the earth's axis remains about the same all of the time, but as the earth orbits around the sun each year, a change in seasons occurs.

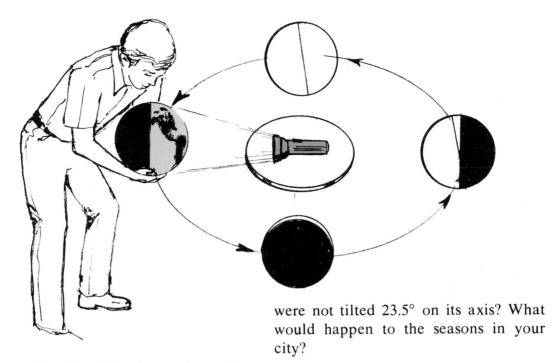

were not tilted 23.5° on its axis? What would happen to the seasons in your city?

For additional information see page 84

Now take the globe for a slow trip around the flashlight (sun). Keep the axis pointed in the same direction as the earth goes into orbit. Stop when you have walked halfway around the "sun." Notice that the southern half of the earth is now getting most of the sun's light. What season is it in the Southern Hemisphere? The south polar region now will have its midnight sun, and the north arctic area will not see the sun for many days. People in the north arctic have long days and a midnight sun during their summer. The sun does not set at all for several days during the summers in both hemispheres.

Repeat the experiment and observe the equatorial zone. How do the days and nights compare here at all seasons? Does this explain why the equatorial zone always has hot weather? What would be the conditions on earth if it

DEFINITIONS

axis — an ideal line extending through the center of a body.

equator — the great circle of the celestial sphere whose plane is perpendicular to the axis of the earth.

inclination — the angle by which anything differs from the perfectly horizontal or vertical, as in the tilt of the earth's axis from the vertical.

Northern Hemisphere — that part of the earth lying north of the equator.

orbit — the path of any object as it revolves about some other object, whether it is the earth's path in revolving around the sun or an electron's path around the nucleus of an atom.

Southern Hemisphere — the southern half of the earth, below the equator.

MAKING A STAR MAP

Cut a large circle out of a sheet of poster board. Divide it into twelve equal pieces as you would in cutting a pie. Moving clockwise, label each section with a calendar month from January to December. Along the outer rim of the circle mark off the days for each month. The map is now ready for charting the constellations as you locate them.

On the first clear night (mark the date on the chart) find an open area where the sky is visible down to the horizon. Face north and locate Polaris. Draw it on the very center of your circle. Fill in the rest of Ursa Minor (the Little Dipper) in the position as you view it. Let's say you are standing in Illinois on November 20. The Little Dipper would be in a position of spilling out. Look to the right and locate the Big Dipper (Ursa Major). Look below and a little to the left to find Draco. Cepheus will be about straight left in line with Ursa Minor. Lyra will be lower in the sky and to the left. Draw in only those constellations you are able to locate.

For greater accuracy draw in concentric circles ten degrees apart from the center out to your dateline. Then use an astrolabe to get the degrees of altitude above the horizon before you draw in a constellation.

Get a commercial star chart for your hemisphere. Compare your map with it. How far off were you on your rough methods of calculating?

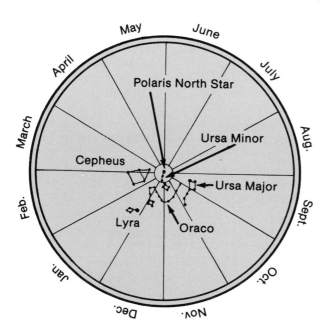

DEFINITIONS

altitude — height above a line used as a base; usually measured from a base of sea level, and expressed in feet and miles or meter and kilometers.

astrolabe — an instrument that measures the exact altitude of stars, used in navigation and surveying; one type has a fixed altitude and depends on exact timing a star reaches that altitude.

concentric circle — a series of circles with a common center, as the ridges in fingerprints or a tree's annual rings.

constellation — any of nearly 100 arbitrary groupings of stars into real or fancied shapes: convenient for locating and identifying stars and other celestial objects.

hemisphere — half of a sphere; half of earth, as the Northern or Southern, Eastern or Western hemisphere.

horizon — the line where the earth appears to meet the sky.

48

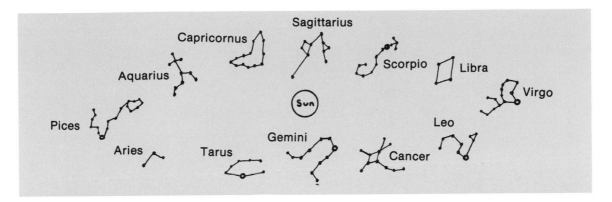

DRAWING THE SIGNS OF THE ZODIAC

The zodiac is a group of twelve constellations that appear to form a circle or band in the sky around an equatorial plane. In the Northern Hemisphere they are visible in the southern sky at different seasons. The circle is designated as 16° wide and at 30° intervals. Ancient people recognized each group of stars, except for one, as animals. Many myths were told about them. Here are the signs: Leo, Virgo, Libra, Scorpio, Sagittarius, Capricorn, Aquarius, Pisces, Aries, Taurus, Gemini, and Cancer.

To better understand and locate these constellations in the night sky, it is helpful to draw the star pattern of each on a large circle of tagboard. Put the sun in the center and the earth to one side with its moon. Use different-sized stars; a constellation often has a very bright star that is given its own name. Then use a series of dots to outline the object or animal it is supposed to resemble. Around the rim of the tagboard, label the months of the year and the time that each sign of the zodiac is visible where you live.

Do some research on the tales about the zodiac. Here is what you would learn about Pisces. It appears in autumn in the Northern Hemisphere. People thought it looked like two fish joined together at their tails by long ribbons outlined by stars. At the end the ribbons form a knot around a bright star. The whole constellation takes the form of an extended and straggling V. Can't you just see someone staring at the night sky, imagining what animal a group of stars look like? Try it yourself. Then see if your friends can spot your creature in the heavens.

Caution: Be sure to hold objects over the flame with tongs.

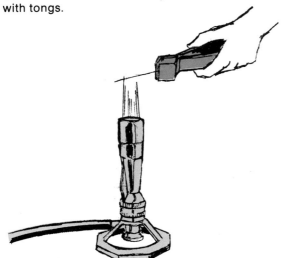

INVESTIGATING STARLIGHT

Our sun is a yellow star with a temperature of more than 10,000° F. Stars three times as hot are bluish white, while those around 5,000° F. are red stars. About what temperatures would orange and yellow-white stars be?

Do the following in order to get an idea of how astronomers arrive at the color and temperature variations of stars. Light a Bunsen burner and adjust the air until the burner has a yellow flame. Light a second burner and adjust the air to a bluish white flame. Place a small beaker half full of water on a tripod over each flame. Time the number of minutes it takes each to boil. What did you find out?

You can also use a very thin iron or steel wire. Hold one end with tongs and place the other end over an open flame. Observe the color of the wire as it gets hotter.

TAKING PICTURES OF STAR TRAILS

For this project you must spend an evening in the open countryside away from the lights of city and highway. The evening sky should be clear of clouds and smog. If you do not have a tripod, take along a box on which to set your camera. Open the diaphragm on the camera to provide the maximum amount of light. Dial the focus to infinity. Look through the camera until you locate Polaris, the North Star, and center it so that all other stars radiate out from this point. Set the shutter speed on time exposure. Push the exposure lever. Do not jar the camera. After exposing the film for one hour, close the shutter carefully.

Using the same procedure, take other time-exposure pictures of the sky in the west, east, and south. Little wedges of wood under the front edge of the camera will tilt it to take pictures at different angles from the horizon. Finally lay the camera on its back and shoot the stars at the zenith position. These would be the stars you would see lying on your back and looking straight up.

After the film is developed, you will end up with a white streak for each star. It appears as if the stars have moved through the sky. How do the star trails taken in the north differ from the ones in the other directions? If the stars aren't moving, what caused the streaks?

For additional information see page 84

DEFINITIONS

diaphragm — a device that controls the amount of light that can hit the film.

horizon — the line where the earth appears to meet the sky.

infinity — any quantity or dimension that has no limiting value; a concept for expressing the increase of any value beyond any assignable limit.

zenith — the area in the sky directly above your head.

with twenty-four lines that represent the longitudes. Each line of longitude equals one hour or 15°, making the full circle of twenty-four hours or 360°.

Use a globe to find the longitude of a particular city. Write it on the corresponding line of your table. As you work with this instrument you will become very proficient at estimating time around the world.

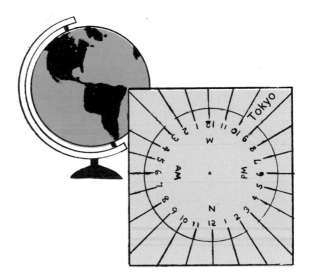

TELLNG TIME AROUND THE WORLD

When it is noon in Chicago, what time is it in London, England, or Sydney, Australia? Mark off a twelve-inch circle into twenty-four equal parts by bisecting the center. Fasten the circle in the center of a large sheet of tagboard with a clip that permits the circle to rotate. Using a yardstick, continue the lines out onto the tagboard so it ends up

DEFINITIONS

bisecting — dividing into two equal parts.

longitude — the angular distance of any point in degrees east or west of a prime meridian running north and south on the earth's surface; the most used prime meridian, selected as 0 degrees, is the Greenwich meridian, and any point on the earth's surface is described in degrees east or west of the prime meridian, up to a maximum of 180 degrees.

rotate — to turn on a center or an axis; the earth's rotation produces day and night.

ASSEMBLING A SPECTROSCOPE

Secure a cardboard tube, such as one found in a roll of paper towels. Cut a circle from an aluminum pie tin. Use a razor blade or sharp knife to cut a half-inch slit in the center. Tape the aluminum to one end of the tube so that no light gets in except through the slit. Make a second circle of cardboard. Cut a half-inch square out the center. Tape a piece of diffraction grating over this square. Diffraction grating can be purchased from most scientific supply companies. Then tape the circle to the other end of the tube. The lines in the grating should parallel the slit at the other end. You now have put together a simple spectroscope.

To use this instrument, look through the grating with the slit pointed at a light source, such as a neon sign, clear light bulb, argon lamp, or other luminous gases. A spectrum will be visible. Each type of gas or chemical element makes its own design. Astronomers use spectroscopes to determine what elements make up objects in the universe.

DEFINITIONS

diffraction — the effect produced when a limited section of a wave front meets a surface; sometimes considered as the bending of light.

spectroscope — an instrument using a prism of diffraction grating to study color lines of the visible spectrum.

spectrum — the colored bands of light produced by passing white or other complex light through a prism or diffraction grating, progressing from the longest visible wave length (red) to the shortest (violet).

CONSTRUCTING A CONSTELLARIUM

A constellarium helps you to learn the star patterns in the sky before attempting to locate them in the dark. The following are a few of the constellations visible in the Northern Hemisphere at various seasons of the year: Big Dipper, Little Dipper, Orion, Perseus, Taurus, Cepheus, Cassiopeia, Hercules, Bootes, Draco, Gemini, and Auriga.

Cut out the center of a round oatmeal or ice cream carton lid. Leave a one-fourth inch frame around the edge. Cut several cardboard disks so that they fit tightly into the lid. Punch out a constellation pattern in each disk. Make larger holes for the brighter stars in each group. Cut a hole in the bottom of the carton just large enough for the bulb end of a flashlight to fit into it exactly. Put one of the disks with the pattern of a constellation on it into the lid of the carton and place the lid on the carton. Go into a dark room. Turn the flashlight on and the constellation can be projected onto a dark surface.

Have some friends make constellariums. Get together so each person can project a different constellation on the ceiling at the same time. Can you make the pattern of the night sky as it is normally seen around the North Star?

DEFINITIONS

constellation — any of nearly 100 arbitrary groupings of stars into real or fancied shapes: convenient for locating and identifying stars and other celestial objects.

Northern Hemisphere — that part of the earth lying north of the equator.

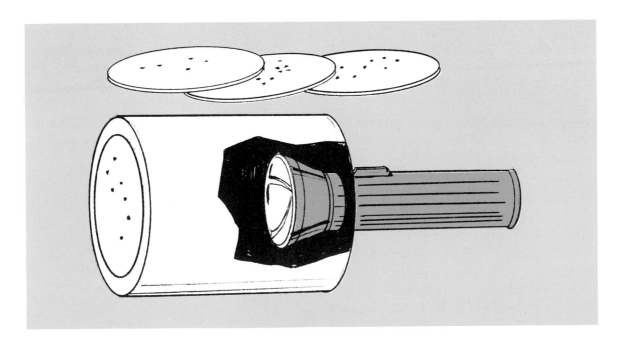

53

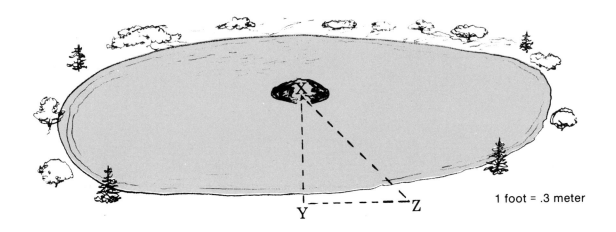

1 foot = .3 meter

MEASURING DISTANCES BY TRIANGULATION

Astronomers use triangles to measure distant objects in space. The following activities, although much too simple for astronomical calculations, still will provide some understanding of how it can be done.

Begin by using the isosceles triangle. Say you want to find the distance of an object which cannot be figured by actually going to it, such as a muskrat home in the middle of a marsh. The home will be labeled X; the place where you are standing on the edge of the marsh will be Y. Put a stick in the ground to mark the spot. Walk to your right in a line that is perpendicular to a line from point Y to point X. When you have reached a place that is at a 45° angle from point X (use a compass), mark the spot as Z. If you have a fairly accurate triangle then you only will

have to measure the distance between Y and Z. This will equal the distance between Y and X.

Another method involves walking out a second triangle. Label the distant object V. The place where you are standing will be W. Walk perpendicular to the right any number of feet, say sixty. Mark the spot and label it X. Continue on the same line for a number of feet, let's say twenty. Mark this spot and label it Y. Make a right turn and walk perpendicularfor several feet, maybe ten, and mark it Z.

You are ready to do your math by using this formula.

$$\frac{V\,W}{W\,X} = \frac{Y\,Z}{X\,Y}$$

How far is the distant object from the spot where you were first standing?

The last method you can do with a partner. Both will need a sheet of paper on a clipboard or other hard surface, a protractor, and a straw for sighting a distant object. Use a telephone pole that is several blocks away. Walk half a block away from each other, making sure both of you keep the pole in view. The distance between you and your partner will be the base of the triangle and can be measured. Set the protractor on the paper with its straight edge in line with the base line. Lay the straw on top of the protractor as you sight through it at the telephone pole. Record the number of degrees where the straw crosses the arc of the protractor. Now with a little geometry you can calculate the distance to the pole using the two angle readings and the length of the baseline.

DEFINITIONS

astronomer — one who is skilled in astronomy or who makes observations of celestial phenomena.

formula — a symbolic expression of the chemical composition or constitution of a substance.

geometry — a branch of mathematics that deals with measurement, properties and relationships of points, lines, angles surfaces, and solids.

perpendicular — standing upright at right angles to plane of the horizon.

protractor — a device shaped in a half circle with 180 degrees marked on it; used to measure angles.

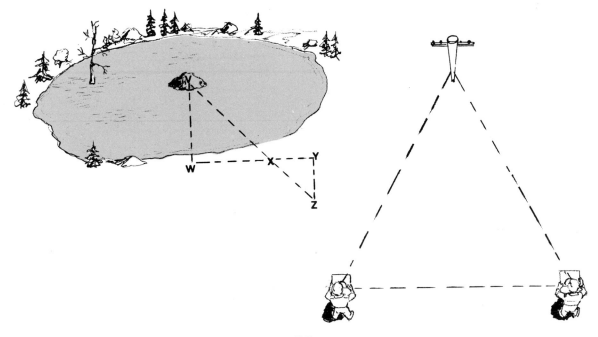

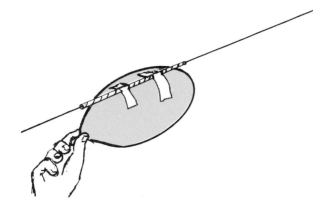

EXPERIMENTING WITH BALLOON ROCKETS

You'll need about fifty feet of fish line. Use black ink to mark five-foot intervals on it. This will make it easier later to measure distances on the line. Anchor one end to a high object—the branch of a tree or the top of a garage door—or tie it inside a second-story window with the rest hanging out. Select several round and oblong balloons, all of different sizes. Blow up one balloon, recording its size and shape. Hold the open end shut while a partner tapes on a drinking straw parallel with the open end. Thread the fish line through the straw so that the mouth of the balloon is pointed away from the anchored end of the line. Hold the free end of the line taut and close to ground level. On the countdown of zero, release the balloon and your "rocket" will blast off. Measure how far the balloon traveled up the line. Continue experimenting with all of the balloons. Keep a record of their sizes when blown up, their shapes, and the distances they rocketed into space.

Can you draw any conclusions as to why scientists designed real rockets as they did? What causes a rocket to go up? What type of "fuel" did you use? What creates the thrust in real rockets? How far and fast must they go to escape earth's gravity and get out into space?

For additional information see page 84

DEFINITIONS

gravity — the gravitional force between the earth and a body near it.

thrust — the force exerted by moving gases that pushes a spacecraft forward; created by ejected burning fuel as in jet and rocket engines.

SETTING UP AN ASTROLABE

Fasten the ends of two 1/2" X 1" X 10" strips of wood together with an elbow hinge. Nail half of the baseline of a plastic protractor on the side of one strip at the hinge end. The attached strip when held upright should be on the 90° mark of the protractor.

You will need a partner to help use your homemade astrolabe in determining the number of degrees on the protractor. On a clear evening locate Polaris, the North Star. Hold the baseline stick parallel to the ground and at eye level. Bend the upright stick at an angle in line with your eye and Polaris. Have your partner read the degree on the protractor where the stick passes. This is the altitude above the horizon.

See if you can locate these stars and then figure their altitude: Capella in the constellation Auriga, Castor in Gemini, Vega in Lyra, Deneb in the Northern Cross, Altair in Aquilla, Regulus in Leo, and Arcturus in Bootes.

DEFINITIONS

astrolabe — an instrument that measures the exact altitude of stars, used in navigation and surveying; one type has a fixed altitude and depends on exact timing a star reaches that altitude.

parallel — equally distant at all places.

Polaris — the bright star seen in Northern Hemisphere that is almost directly above the earth's northern axis, also called the North Star.

protractor — a device shaped in a half circle with 180 degrees marked on it; used to measure angles.

1 inch = 2.5 centimeters

WORKING WITH LATITUDE AND LONGITUDE

A globe is marked off with east-west lines of latitude and north-south lines of longitude. Each line marks a 15° interval, about seventy miles apart. Lines of longitude also are an hour apart in time.

To locate a place on the earth and what time it is there at any given moment, build a simplified model of a globe. Purchase a large white ball or

blow up a round balloon and cover it with one-half inch of papier-mâché to represent the earth. Use a string to measure its circumference. Divide the string into twenty-four equal parts, marking the string at these places. Tape the string around the globe at its ends. Tack the ends of a strip of heavy cardboard at both poles while you draw the lines of longitude around the globe. Repeat the procedure by drawing lines at right angles to these for the lines of latitude.

Select one longitude and label it 0°,

which is the prime meridian that passes through Greenwich, England. Moving east and west label each longitude 15° apart. The line directly opposite 0° should be 180°. Do the same for the latitude lines, with the equator being 0°.

Now begin to place towns and cities of interest to you in their proper locations. Chicago is at about 42° latitude and 88° longitude, while Los Angeles is at around 34° latitude and 118° longitude. What is the time difference? What well-known city in a southern state is at around 26° latitude and 80° longitude? Locate the capital of a cold state located at 58° latitude and 135° longitude. Working with these imaginary lines on earth will enable you to become an armchair traveler.

DEFINITIONS

circumference — the distance around a circle.

equator — the great circle of the celestial sphere whose plane is perpendicular to the axis of the earth.

latitude — the angular distance of any point north or south of the equator, measured in degrees from the equator, at 0 degrees.

longitude — the angular distance of any point in degrees east or west of a prime meridian running north and south on the earth's surface.

prime meridian — the meridian indicated as 0 degrees, from which longitude east and west is figured; passes through Greenwich, England.

Chapter 3
Weather

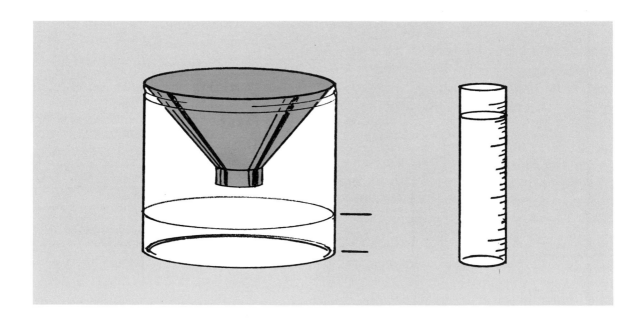

MAKING A
RAIN GAUGE

To determine the exact amount of rainfall in your own backyard, you will need a gauge to measure it. The weatherman's report is an average of rainfall over a larger area of land.

Use a metal or plastic funnel the same diameter as any widemouthed jar with straight sides. Rainfall is so slight sometimes that it is difficult to measure the water collected in a large container. So figure out the same quantity in a narrow bottle. Put an inch of water into the large jar. Measure it with a ruler. Now pour this into a tall thin bottle which has the same diameter the entire length of the bottle. Make a mark at the water level. Mark this "inch" into eight equal parts. Do the same for the second and third inches.

Set the funnel in the large jar out in an open area away from trees and other obstructions. Immediately after a rainstorm bring the jar in and pour it into the tall measuring gauge. This enables you to read fractions of an inch.

CAUSING DEW AND FROST TO FORM

Remove the paper jacket from a tin can. Fill the can with one cup of water and one cup of broken ice cubes. Add one-half cup of table or rock salt. Stir the mixture vigorously. Set a thermometer in the can. Record the air temperature in the room at the time you begin the experiment. At what temperature do droplets of water collect on the outside of the can? Where does this moisture come from? This is the dew point for the temperature at the time of the experiment. As soon as the drops freeze you have created frost. What can you conclude if the temperature of the air is close to the dew point reading? Repeat this activity on different days and in various locations inside and outdoors. Explain your results.

For additional information see page 84

ice water

hot water in glass

MAKING WATER BOIL BY COOLING

Pour water into a heatproof glass bottle to the halfway mark. Place the bottle in a pan of water on the stove. Heat until the water in the bottle has boiled for at least five minutes. Turn it off, or remove it from the source of heat. The water will stop boiling. Immediately cap the bottle and turn it upside down in a pan of water. (Wear gloves so you don't burn your fingers.) Slowly pour a glass of ice water over the bottle. Does the water start to boil again? Why? To help answer this problem, consider the difference in air pressure. Does this explain why it takes longer to cook a meal in the mountains than in a valley?

For additional information see page 84

For additional information see page 85

MAKING A RAINBOW

Rainbows can be made by holding a prism in sunlight and letting the rays hit a white wall. Sun hitting an aquarium will cast a rainbow on the opposite side. A glass of water on a windowsill will direct the sun's rays into a spectrum on the inside. The most effective and realistic way to make a rainbow is to take a water hose into the backyard in early morning or late afternoon. With your back to the sun, shoot the water into a dark background, such as a building or clump of trees. The water drops will reflect the light and break it up into the color spectrum.

Have you ever seen a double rainbow? In which directions are the colors arranged? Can you explain the flip-flop of the spectrum in one of them? Is it the higher or lower rainbow in the sky that reverses itself?

DISCOVERING FACTORS THAT AFFECT THE FREEZING POINT OF LIQUIDS

Put a layer of chipped ice on the bottom of a metal pail. Rest a small tin can filled with milk on this layer. Keep adding chipped ice around the can until it is level with the top. Put a circle of

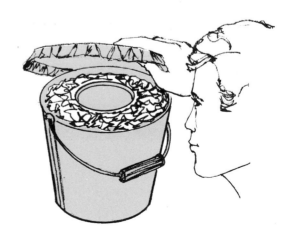

aluminum foil over the whole surface. Occasionally observe the condition of the can. How long does it take the milk to start freezing?

Repeat the experiment a second time. This time sprinkle several tablespoons of rock or table salt on every inch-high layer of ice chips. How long does it take the milk to freeze now? Why? For a solid to be changed to a liquid, heat is necessary. Where does the heat come from?

Fill a pint jar with colored water and cap it. Set the jar in a bucket of chipped ice, salt, and water. Watch the liquid carefully. Just before it appears to reach the freezing point remove the cap. What does this do to the pressure in the jar? What happened to the liquid when the cap was removed?

For additional information see page 85

1 inch = 2.5 centimeters

MEASURING SNOWFALL

Mark inches on a coffee can starting at the bottom. Place the can outside away from buildings and trees when a snowfall has been forecast. When it stops snowing, record the number of inches of snow in the can. Check the reading by letting the snow melt.

How many inches of snow will make an inch of water? It will take several snowfalls to determine the answer. Each time it snows, set the same can outside to collect snow. Record the number of inches and type of snowflakes. Were they fine and fluffy or large, heavy flakes? Let the snow melt at room temperature and remeasure the amount of water in the can. After you have collected data from several snowfalls, figure the ratio of snow to water.

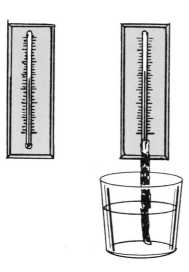

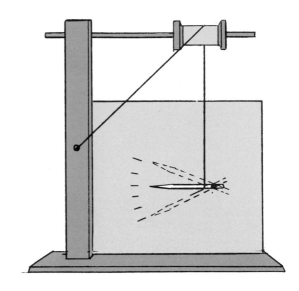

CONSTRUCTING HYGROMETERS

Here are directions for setting up a wet-and-dry-bulb hygrometer to calculate relative humidity. Since commercial thermometers (not clinical ones) do not always agree, select two that are recording the same temperature in the store before you purchase them. Suspend them from a support. Cut the metal or plastic ends off a shoestring. Put one cut end of the shoestring over the bulb of the thermometer that will be designated the wet bulb. Place the other end of the shoestring in a glass of water. To determine the relative humidity for any particular day, figure the difference in the readings of the dry-and-wet-bulb thermometers. Using the chart, you will find an approximate answer. For example, if the wet-bulb reading is 70° and the dry-bulb reading is 80°, the difference in the readings is 10°. Find the dry-bulb temperature and the 10° dif-

ference on the chart. The approximate relative humidity is seen to be 55 percent in this case.

A crude indicator of moisture difference in the air can be set up in the following manner. Use a long, straight, blond, freshly washed hair. Construct a wooden stand similar to the one in the picture. Find a spool and dowel which fit together tightly so that the spool turns fairly easily without falling off. Fasten the hair to a tack on the side of the stand and run it over the spool. Make a cardboard scale and attach it to the base of the stand. Cut the end of a large drinking straw to a point and attach it to the scale with a pintack. The straw must be free to move. The section in front of the pintack should be slightly longer and heavier than the section behind the pintack. Suspend the heavy part of the straw by tying the hair around it.

Now wet a towel with hot water and place it over the instrument for a few minutes. Remove it and quickly mark

TEMPERATURE DIFFERENCES BETWEEN
READINGS OF WET AND DRY BULBS

C°		.6°	1.1°	1.7°	2.2°	2.8°	3.3°	3.9°	4.4°	5.0°	5.6°	6.1°	6.7°	7.2°	7.8°
	F°	1°	2°	3°	4°	5°	6°	7°	8°	9°	10°	11°	12°	13°	14°
17.8°	64°	95	90	84	79	74	70	65	60	56	51	47	43	38	34
18.3°	65°	95	90	85	80	75	71	66	61	57	53	48	44	40	36
18.9°	66°	95	90	85	80	75	71	66	61	57	53	48	44	40	36
19.4°	67°	95	90	85	80	75	71	66	62	58	53	49	45	41	37
20°	68°	95	90	85	80	76	71	67	62	58	54	50	46	42	38
20.6°	69°	95	90	85	81	76	72	67	63	59	55	51	47	43	39
21.1°	70°	95	90	86	81	77	72	68	64	59	55	51	48	44	40
21.7°	71°	95	90	86	81	77	72	68	64	60	56	52	48	45	41
22.2°	72°	95	91	86	82	77	73	69	65	61	57	53	49	45	42
22.8°	73°	95	91	86	82	78	73	69	65	61	57	53	50	46	42
23.3°	74°	95	91	86	82	78	74	69	65	61	58	54	50	47	43
23.8°	75°	96	91	86	82	78	74	70	66	62	58	54	51	47	44
24.4°	76°	96	91	87	82	78	74	70	66	62	59	55	51	48	44
25°	77°	96	91	87	83	79	74	71	67	63	59	56	52	48	45
25.6°	78°	96	91	87	83	79	75	71	67	63	60	56	53	49	46
26.1°	79°	96	91	87	83	79	75	71	68	64	60	57	53	50	46
26.7°	80°	96	91	87	83	79	75	72	68	64	61	57	54	50	47

where the straw is pointing on the scale. This will indicate high humidity. The hair should have stretched, allowing the pointer to fall. Now make the hair very, very dry by placing the instrument near a radiator, hot-air vent, or furnace for several hours. Mark the spot where the straw is pointing. It should be toward the top of the scale. This mark indicates low humidity. This instrument will not give you an exact relative-humidity reading, but it will indicate changes in the humidity.

To make a chemical hygrometer, first purchase a small jar of cobalt chloride crystals. Dissolve enough crystals in a half cup of water to color it a deep red. Cut several flags out of white cotton cloth and soak them in this solution. Locate an equal number of dowel rods or sticks to act as flagpoles. Staple each flag to the top of a pole. The poles are now ready to be driven into the ground in a variety of places—the sunny side of a building, a shady location, an open area subject to wind currents, along the bank of a stream, in the woods or under a big tree, inside a house or classroom. Hourly or daily observe any color changes in the flags. What color is a flag that is completely dry? Use the data collected and draw conclusions about humidity under a wide variety of conditions.

DEFINITIONS

hygrometer — an instrument for calculating humidity, the amount of water in the air or in other substances; one type depends on expansion and contraction of organic materials, such as hair, with change in moisture content.

relative humidity — the ratio of the amount of water vapor actually present in the air to the greatest amount possible at the same temperature.

65

COMPARING TEMPERATURES OF WET AND DRY AIR

This experiment must be done on a windy day. Hang a wet towel on a clothesline with the wind hitting the towel broadside. Take the temperature of the air at least ten feet off to the side of the wet towel. Record the number of degrees. Take a second reading a couple of feet in front of the towel so that the wind is blowing in your face. What is the temperature here? Explain the difference in relation to humidity.

For additional information see page 85

EXPERIMENTING WITH CONDENSATION

Place a pitcher of ice water in a warm room. Observe what happens on the outside of the pitcher. Would coloring the ice water prove that the droplets on the outside did not come from within the container?

Hold a tray of ice cubes above the steam from a kettle. Be careful. Where did the water forming on the underside of the tray come from? Why do cold water pipes drip in the summer? What happens when you blow on a cold windowpane? Does cold or hot air hold more moisture? What do you see when you open a freezer door on a hot, humid summer day? What happens to the mirror in the bathroom when you take a hot shower? Would the amount of moisture that accumulates depend upon the amount of humidity on a particular day?

For additional information see page 85

DEFINITIONS

condensation — change from the gaseous to the liquid state, produced by removal of heat from the gas.

CAUTION: THIS EXPERIMENT SHOULD BE DONE WITH ADULT SUPERVISION.

USING THE BEAUFORT WIND SCALE

The Beaufort scale indicates wind speed in chart form. It uses the effect of wind on objects to describe wind speed. It is not as precise as the anemometer, but it still is used occasionally by weather stations. The scale was devised by Sir Francis Beaufort. Copy the scale on a large poster board that can be hung in your weather station for quick reference. Illustrations on your chart will help make it clearer and more interesting. By watching the effects of wind you can estimate its speed.

Number 3 on the Beaufort Wind Scale is a gentle breeze. Flags fly in this wind.

Number 5 on the Beaufort Wind Scale is called a fresh breeze. Small trees sway in this wind.

DEFINITIONS

anemometer — an instrument for measuring wind speed; usually a cup anemometer, with three cups mounted on a shaft.

NUMBER	TITLE	EFFECT OF WIND	MILES PER HOUR
0	calm	smoke rises vertically	less than 1
1	light air	smoke drifts	1-3
2	light breeze	leaves rustle	4-7
3	gentle breeze	flags fly	8-12
4	moderate breeze	dust and loose paper are raised	13-18
5	fresh breeze	small trees sway	19-24
6	strong breeze	difficult to use umbrellas	25-31
7	moderate gale	difficult to walk	32-38
8	fresh gale	twigs break off trees	39-46
9	strong gale	slight damage to roofs	47-54
10	whole gale	trees uprooted	55-63
11	storm	widespread damage	64-75
12	hurricane	devastation	above 75

DEFINITIONS

convection — the flow of heat from one place to another, caused by convection current (mass movements of heated particles) in liquids and gases.

molecule — the smallest particle of a substance that retains the properties of the substance and is composed of one or more atoms.

For additional information see page 85

PRODUCING CONVECTIONS IN AIR

Construct a small wooden box about six inches high, ten inches long, and eight inches wide. Cut a piece of clear plastic six inches by ten inches for one of the sides. Cut out two holes in the top of the box slightly smaller than the size of the two chimneys you are using. Chimneys can be made by cutting off the bottoms and necks of two clear plastic bottles. Follow the adjoining illustration in assembling a convection box.

Place a lighted candle inside the box under one hole. Fasten the plastic sheet across the open side of the box with masking tape. Ignite a dampened rolled-paper towel to cause it to smolder. The towel should be wet enough so it will not flame up. Hold it over the chimney that is not over the candle. Observe the path of smoke. Think about hot air, cold air, and molecule movement to explain what is happening.

ice

MAKING FOG

Fill a beaker with boiling water and let it sit for several minutes. Pour off all but a couple of inches of the water. Place a chunk on ice on top on the mouth of the beaker. After several minutes observe what is happening above the surface of the water. Would you get the same results if you used cold water? Repeat the experiment and make a conclusion.

For additional information see page 86

MAKING A CLOUD

Drill a hole in the center of a cork that fits snugly into the mouth of a jar. Insert a plastic tube into the hole in the cork. Rinse the inside of the jar with one-fourth cup of water mixed with one-fourth cup of alcohol. Pour out the liquid, leaving the inside of the jar wet. Add several pinches of finely crushed blackboard chalk. Put the cork with the tube into the neck of the jar.

Blow through the tube to scatter the chalk and compress the air. Now quickly suck very hard on the tube. Does the temperature of the air go up or down when it is compressed? Does cold or warm air hold more moisture? Explain what happened inside the jar as you drew some of the air out of it.

For additional information see page 86

MEASURING HEAT ABSORPTION

Cut six-inch squares of different colored poster board or construction paper. Include one white and one black square. Waterproof them with varnish or laminate them in plastic. Get some rulers, one more than the number of squares. The experiment must be done on a sunny winter day when the ground is covered with snow. Select a level area of snow on which to place the pieces of colored paper. Push a ruler into the snow to the same depth beside each piece. Push the last ruler in an uncovered spot. This is a control. Each hour record any changes you observe. Which color absorbs the most heat? Which is the best reflector?

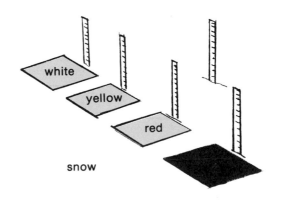

EXPERIMENTING WITH AIR

Turn a small open bottle upside down in a large bottle of water. Push down on the cork of the big bottle. Water forces the air inside the inverted floating bottle to become compressed. The volume of water displaced by the bottle is decreased. The buoyant force is decreased. What happens to the bottle? When the cork is removed, what does the bottle do?

Turn two glasses upside down and push them below the surface of the water in an aquarium. Tilt one glass to permit it to fill with water. Hold the glasses next to each other with the rim of the glass filled with air slightly below the rim of the other glass. Now tilt the glass of air to allow the air to escape. As the second glass catches the bubbles, what happens to the water?

Crumple a sheet of paper and push it into the bottom of a drinking glass. Turn the glass over and push it straight down into a large jar or bowl of water. Does the paper get wet? Does air take up space?

Crumple a sheet of paper and drop it into a milk bottle. Since milk bottles are becoming antiques, you may have to use a similar glass bottle. Make sure the opening is slightly smaller than the diameter of an egg. Light the end of a paper drinking straw. Hold the burning end in the bottle until the paper catches on fire. Let the paper burn until the flame goes out. Set a hard-boiled egg with the shell removed and the pointed end down over the opening of the bottle. Watch what happens to the egg. What causes the egg to do this? Can you figure out a way to get the egg out?

This experiment is best done outside or over a sink. Fill a drinking glass or

plastic cup with water. Place a square of cardboard, several inches wider than the glass, on top of the glass. Hold it in place and invert. Carefully move your hand away. What happens to the cardboard? What is holding it in place? Would it work with one half of a glass of water? One third of a glass of water? Other liquids?

This next experiment will work only if you can find a free or inexpensive yardstick that breaks easily. A strip of scrap wood also will work. Lay the stick on a table or counter top so that almost half of it extends out over the edge. Place several sheets of newspaper over the part that is resting on the table. Standing to the side and using the side of your hand, strike the stick at a spot just an inch or two from the edge of the table. Be sure no one is in line with the stick. If the wood is too hard, it will not break and fly off into the air. How can a few sheets of paper hold one half of the stick down despite such a blow on the other half?

Can air crush a can so that it looks as if a truck ran over it? You will need a tin or aluminum gallon can with a screw cap. Empty duplicator-fluid cans can be obtained in many schools. Some products in grocery stores come in similar cans. Be sure to wash out and air dry any container you use. Now put one-half inch or one-half cup of water into the can. Place it on a heat source until the water is boiling vigorously. Remove it from the heat and quickly screw on the cap. In a minute or two you will see and hear what happens to the can. It has to do with the difference in air pressure. Can you explain the action inside and outside?

For additional information see page 86

DEFINITIONS

compressed — increased pressure in or on any system or part.

displaced — a change in position from that previously occupied by a body.

invert — to turn upside down.

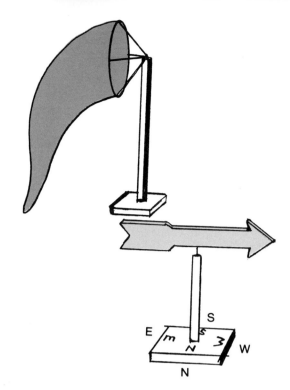

finger. Drill a hole in one end of a thick dowel rod. Fasten the dowel upright to a wooden base or drive it directly into the ground near your weather station. Oil the hole in the dowel before setting the arrow onto the stand. This will reduce friction as the wind vane turns with the breeze. Use a compass to mark the base with the directions before setting it up outside. If the point of the arrow swings to the north, then the wind is a north wind.

SETTING UP WIND DIRECTIONAL DEVICES

A wind sock can be made by sewing a piece of cotton mesh or lightweight cloth in the shape of a cone. Fasten the wide mouth of the cone to a stiff wire circle. Nail a dowel rod to a wooden base for the support. With string tie the cone on the upper end of the rod. Use a compass to determine exact directions. Paint the letters N, S, E, and W on the base of the support when you have it in its permanent setting.

To assemble a wind vane, saw an arrow out of a piece of wood an inch thick and about eight inches long. Hammer a long spike from the center of the top edge through to the underside. The spike should protrude two inches. Determine where the center of gravity is on the arrow by balancing it on your

ASSEMBLING BAROMETERS

To set up a mercurial barometer, you will have to seal the end of a three-foot glass tube by rotating it gently over a hot flame. Tilt the tube at a slight angle as you slowly fill it with mercury. Shake the tube gently, or run a fine wire down the tube if bubbles of air separate the column of mercury. Use rubber gloves while you are working with this chemical. Place a finger over the open end, invert the tube, and submerge the end in a small dish of mercury. Follow the illustration in designing a support to hold the barometer.

Air pressure is about fifteen pounds per square inch at sea level. The mercury column will stay about thirty inches high. General weather changes can be predicted by watching the level of mercury rise and fall. If water were used, it would require a thirty-two-foot

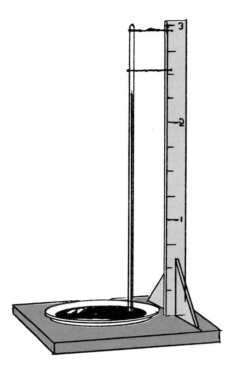

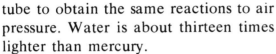

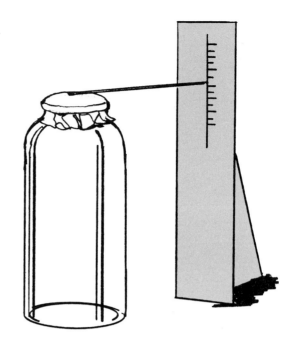

tube to obtain the same reactions to air pressure. Water is about thirteen times lighter than mercury.

To make a simple aneroid barometer (no liquid), fasten a circle of rubber from a balloon over the top of a bottle. Tape it securely in place. Glue one end of a broom straw to the center of the rubber cap. Place a cardboard or poster board scale at the free end of the straw so that it is close but doesn't touch. Choose a clear day. Obtain the correct air pressure from a newspaper or television weather forecast. Use this pressure reading as a starting point to make the scale.

As air pressure increases, the rubber is pushed down into the bottle and the other end of the straw goes up. Temperature, too, has an effect on the rubber top, so keep the instrument in a place that has a fairly steady temperature.

In a regular commercial aneroid barometer, a thin metal case surrounds the instrument. Part of the air is removed from inside the case. As air pressure changes, the walls of the case move in or out and the internal instruments indicate the changes on a dial.

DEFINITIONS

aneroid barometer — a barometer in which the action of atmospheric pressure in bending a metallic surface is made to move a pointer.

barometer — an instrument for measuring pressure, usually air pressure.

sea level — the level of the surface of the sea especially as its mean position midway between mean high and low water.

WORKING WITH THERMOMETERS

Using weather and soil thermometers, one can record temperatures in a variety of places. Make a prediction each time as to the degree of change under each condition. Here are a few suggestions: in full sun, in a shaded area, the surface of a sandy beach, six inches into the sand, shallow water, deep water (tie a rock and string to your thermometer), surface of the soil, six inches into the soil, outside a window at the top of a tall building, under a pile of decaying leaves or grass cuttings, top of a snowbank, several feet under the snow, before and after a rainstorm. How close were your predictions? Explain the reasons for the rise or fall of temperature in each location.

How does the degree of absorption affect temperature? Cover one weather thermometer with a black cloth. Cover a second one with a white cloth. Set both thermometers in the sun for one-half hour. Which thermometer registers a higher temperature? Does the black or white cloth absorb more light and therefore more heat?

Make an air thermometer by following these directoins. Obtain two empty baby food jars or similar containers. Drill a hole in a cork for one of the jars. Insert a section of plastic tubing through the hole. You can use modeling clay around the tubing if you are careful

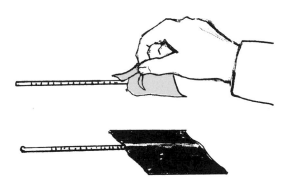

to make it airtight. Fill the second bottle with colored water. Invert the bottle with the stopper over the second bottle so that the end of the plastic tube is in the solution. Fasten this apparatus to a wooden support.

A scale may be made from the readings of a commercial thermometer. Set your thermometer outside in full sunshine. When the temperature rises, does the fluid go up or come down in the tube? Does air expand or contract when it gets colder?

For additional information see page 87

DEFINITIONS

contract — to shrink or reduce in size.

expand — to increase in volume or size.

CONSTRUCTING AN ANEMOMETER

Cut two hollow rubber balls in half. Assemble the materials according to the illustration. Nail the halves of the balls on the ends of the two sticks. In the top of the wooden support drill a hole a little larger than the nail used in the cross arms. Oil the inside of the hole to cut down on friction. Paint one cup a different color to make counting easier. To determine wind velocity (miles per hour), count the number of revolutions in thirty seconds and divide by five.

A more accurate method is to calibrate the revolutions with the speedometer of a moving car. On a calm day have someone drive a car at ten miles an hour while you hold the anemometer out the window of the passenger side. Count the number of revolutions per minute. Repeat this at twenty miles per hour. Record the turns and arrive at an average figure.

If the anemometer is mounted on a stake several feet high, it can be driven into the ground in an open area. It is an essential device in a weather station.

DEFINITIONS

anemometer — an instrument for measuring wind speed; usually a cup anemometer, with three cups mounted on a shaft.

calibrate — to determine and verify a scale of values in an instrument, as a thermometer, so that readings can be made and measurements taken.

friction — the force of resistance a body offers to motion, produced by its contact with another body; may be rolling friction, as with wheels or ball bearings on a surface, or sliding friction, as with a box being dragged over a surface.

velocity — the rate of motion (speed) of a body in a given direction; velocity equals distance divided by time.

DISCOVERING FACTORS RELATED TO EVAPORATION

Find out what type of soil loses water most quickly by evaporation. Fill four pots of the same size with these soils: sand, clay, loam, and peat. Record the weight of each pot of soil. Record the weight of one cup of water. Pour one cup of water into each pot of soil. Set all four pots in the sun. Weigh the pots daily until all are down to their original weights. Which one took the longest to lose all its water? What affects the rate of evaporation—the color or the texture of the soil? How does this information affect a choice in the types of soil that would be best for gardening or farming?

Now pour a cup of water in a pan and set it to one side. Pour a cup of water in a second pan. Place this one over a source of heat for half an hour. Measure the amount of water left in both pans. What does heat do to water molecules and the rate of evaporation?

Pour a cup of water in each of three different-sized containers—an olive jar, a bowl, and a cake pan. Let these stand for one week. Measure the amount of water left in each container. Explain the results.

Place an electric fan in front of a pan containing one cup of water. Put another pan with an equal amount of water on the far side of the room. Turn on the fan for one hour. Measure the amount of liquid in the two pans. Which has less? What effect does wind have on humidity and evaporation?

For additional information see page 87

DEFINITIONS

evaporation — the process of passing off in vapor or in invisible minute particles.

humidity — a moderate degree of wetness in the atmosphere.

molecule — the smallest particle of a substance that retains the properties of the substance and is composed of one or more atoms.

CALCULATING THE SPEED OF SOUND AND LIGHTNING

Watch the sky during a thunderstorm. The instant you see lightning start counting off the seconds by saying "one thousand and one, one thousand and two, one thousand and three," and so on, until you hear the clap of thunder. If you have counted up to five seconds, the storm is one mile away. If you reach thirty seconds, it is six miles away.

Keep counting periodically. You will be able to tell whether the storm is coming closer or moving away by the decreasing or increasing number of seconds. Sound travels about one-fiftieth of a mile per second and light travels 186,000 miles per second.

KEEPING A DAILY CHART OF WEATHER

Use a large piece of plywood as a background. Divide the bottom ten inches of the plywood into thirty-five two-inch squares. Screw an L-hook into the top of each square. In the space above the squares put a row of L-hooks to hold the name of the month and the year. The top of the plywood has room for a suitable illustration for each month of the year. The hooks on either side of it hold extra cards.

Make many two-inch cardboard squares, each with a hole in the top. You'll need enough letters to spell all the months, cards with numbers from 1 to 31, a card for every day of the week, and extra numbers for the year.

At the beginning of each month, arrange the dates properly under the days of the week. Each day, make a symbol out of colored construction paper to indicate the kind of weather on that day. You might use an umbrella for rain, a yellow sun for a clear day, etc. Use your imagination! Hang the paper weather symbols on the hooks over the cards that show the dates.

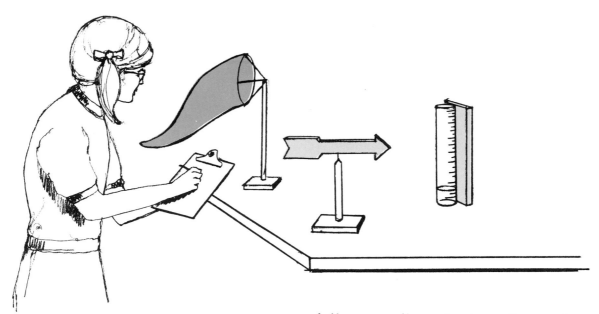

daily recording chart. Remember that these recordings are only approximate readings. Check with daily newspapers for comparisons.

RECORDING AND PREDICTING WEATHER

To set up a weather station you will have to construct instruments. Background information and instructions for making the following devices and weather conditions are found in this book: anemometer, barometer, Beaufort scale, clouds, convection, evaporation, fog, frost, hygrometer, rain gauge, precipitation, snow gauge, thermometers, and wind directional devices.

Place the anemometer, rain gauge, and snow gauge in an open area away from buildings and trees. Other instruments should be housed in shelters, free from the elements. Prepare a Beaufort scale and other charts from information gathered from the entries mentioned above, and keep with the

DEFINITIONS

anemometer — an instrument for measuring wind speed; usually a cup anemometer, with three cups mounted on a shaft.

barometer — an instrument for measuring pressure, usually air pressure.

convection — the flow of heat from one place to another, caused by convection current (mass movements of heated particles) in liquids and gases.

evaporation — the process of passing off in vapor or in invisible minute particles.

hygrometer — any of several instruments for measuring the humidity of the atmosphere.

precipitation — moisture condensed from the air, as rain, snow, sleet, dew.

COLLECTING AIR POLLUTANTS

What causes smog? What is the pollen count on a particular day? No matter where you live, there will always be particles in the air from industry, plants, automobiles, airplanes, and activities that people engage in during work and play. Here's how to take a reading on the air pollutants in your locality.

Coat one side of a number of microscopic slides with white petroleum jelly or a similar grease or oil. On a windy day set the slides outside in various locations: the window sill of a house in the country, outside an apartment building in a large city, on the side of a busy highway, at a corner by a stoplight or stop sign, in a meadow, in a forest, on a beach, outside a factory, along a roadside that has not been mowed. Tape one end of the slide and give it a number. Record the number, location, and conditions at each spot. After a given amount of time, half an hour or longer, collect the slides and study them with a strong hand lens or microscope. Tabulate the number and relative size of all particulates. You will find particles of soil, soot, sand, pollen, and other pollutants stuck in the oil film on the slides. Which areas contain the greatest number and variety of foreign materials? Which location is the healthiest for breathing fresh, clean air?

DEFINITIONS

particulates — small, separate particles.

smog — a suspension of smoke, fog, and dust in air, particularly from industrial processes and automobile exhausts.

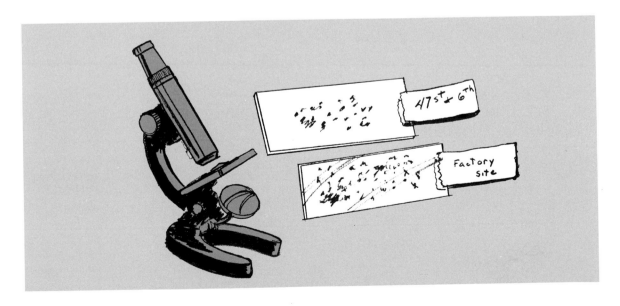

SETTING UP A NEPHOSCOPE

A nephoscope is a device used to track the directional movement of clouds. On a street in the heart of a big city the wind direction can change because of many surface obstructions. To get the true wind direction over a city, it is best to note where the clouds are moving.

Get a large mirror and a grease pencil or marker that will write on glass. Go outside in an open area on a windy day with scattered clouds in the sky. Set the mirror on the ground. Using a compass, mark the four directions on the sides of the mirror. Sit down and watch the mirror for cloud reflections to appear. Put an X in the center of a cloud as it appears on the edge of the mirror. Continue to put X's as it moves from one side to the other. Join the X's with a line and determine which direction the cloud took. This is a more accurate wind indicator than a wind sock or vane on the ground. Winds are classified by the direction from which they are coming, not the direction in which they are going.

DEFINITIONS

nephoscope — an instrument for observing the direction and velocity of clouds.

Appendix

Chapter 1

MAKING SOIL page 9

Air and water can change or weather rocks to produce soil. Changes in temperature, freezing, and thawing cause rocks to crack and crumble. The acid given off by growing plants will erode rocks to produce soil. Oxidation occurs as oxygen in the air reacts with minerals in a rock to form oxides which are often water soluble. The glaciers that moved over the earth produced much of the soil present today. A two-mile-high ice glacier could pulverize boulders into bits.

CONSERVING TOPSOIL page 13

Barren soil on a hillside erodes the fastest. When crops are planted in rows going down a, hill water will erode the soil in between the rows. Contour planting of crops around a hill does the best job in conserving topsoil. The fibrous root systems of plants in the grass family form a barrier for water runoff.

DETERMINING WATER RETENTION OF SOILS page 14

Gravel and sand are large particles that have many pockets of air. This allows water to flow through rapidly. Loam is a mixture of sand, clay, silt, and humus. When it is mixed and has more sand than clay, its porosity increases. Clay soil is composed of the finest particles. Water adheres to each particle and cements them together. When clay hardens one can make bricks and pottery. It does not provide a good medium for healthy plant growth.

DETERMINING FACTORS NECESSARY FOR HUMUS BREAKDOWN page 15

Fungi and bacteria are the two groups of plants that decompose dead organic material and return minerals and nutrients to the soil. Most of these organisms function best in warm, dark, and moist places.

Appendix

FINDING OUT ABOUT BUOYANCY page 17

Archimedes' principle states that a solid object when immersed in a liquid is buoyed up by a force equal to the weight of the displaced liquid. One cubic foot of fresh water weighs about 62.3 pounds.

MEASURING THE POROSITY OF SOILS page 18

Usually ground that has been compacted, such as on a ball diamond, does not have loose, aerated soil which will permit water to percolate through readily. A meadow or lawn has soil filled with growing roots and burrowing animal life which increase its porosity. Good soil or loam for optimum plant growth has a combination of sand, silt, clay, and humus.

WEATHERING ROCKS page 26

Heat causes rocks to expand while cold causes them to contract. Sedimentary rocks are softer and more porous than metamorphic and igneous, therefore weathering is faster. Water causes some minerals to go into solution. This produces cracks in the rock or fragments that are washed away.

Lichens and mosses produce acids as they cling to rocks. This pH condition slowly disintegrates rocks, crumbling them into soil particles.

CREATING A DELTA page 31

Deltas are formed as the waters in a fast-moving river slow down when they meet a relatively still body of water, such as the ocean. The coarse heavy particles, such as rocks, pebbles, and sand, settle out first. The finest particles, clay, continue out farther and settle in deeper waters. The Mississippi River forms up to two hundred feet of delta each year. The Nile River forms a huge delta, too.

MAKING STALACTITES AND STALAGMITES page 34

Calcium deposits that form in cone-shaped formations on the floor of a cave are called stalagmites. As water seeps through the limestone roofs of caves it leaves calcium deposits that form into hanging icicles of these compounds. They are called stalactites.

Appendix

Chapter 2

SHOWING THE PHASES OF THE MOON page 39

The first sliver of light on the moon is called the crescent stage. In the first quarter, half of the moon is reflecting sunlight. This takes one week. At the end of two weeks the earth is between the sun and moon. A full moon appears. As the moon makes one full revolution the crescent stage occurs and then the new moon. The moon makes one rotation during one revolution. This is the reason we always see the same side of the moon.

FINDING OUT ABOUT CENTRIFUGAL FORCE page 41

Centrifugal force is the pull of an object which is moving in a circle. Increasing the weight and speed of the moving object will increase the centrifugal force. The centripetal force is exerted by the arm to keep the object from flying out. This is the equal and opposite of centrifugal force.

EXPERIMENTING WITH GRAVITY page 42

Gravity is the force that pulls objects to the earth. Gravity causes an object to accelerate. The object will travel faster and faster the farther it falls.

It was Galileo who discovered that two bodies of different weights when dropped from the same height will reach the ground at the same time. The shape of the objects will be affected by the retarding action of the air. Only in a vacuum will a feather and a bullet reach the bottom at the same time.

MEASURING SHADOWS page 44

The stick will cast a longer shadow in the Northern Hemisphere in the winter months, while during the summer the shadow will be short. During the latter the sun's rays are more directly overhead. This position also raises the temperature.

DEMONSTRATING ECLIPSES page 44

A lunar eclipse occurs when the earth comes between the moon and sun. The earth causes a shadow to form on the lunar surface. To see a lunar eclipse you have your back to the sun while looking at the moon. The moon's revolution around the earth follows an orbit whose plane is slightly inclined to the plane of the earth's orbit. Only periodically are they lined up so that the earth blocks the sun's rays.

Appendix

EXPLAINING SEASONS page 46

When the light hits the upper half of the ball the Northern Hemisphere is having summer. When the rays are on the equator it is fall. As the earth revolves and more light is directed on the bottom half of the ball the upper half or Northern Hemisphere is having winter. On the last quarter of a turn in one complete revolution light again hits the equator bringing spring to the north. If the earth were not tilted on its axis there would be no change of seasons. The climate at the equator stays pretty constant.

TAKING PICTURES OF STAR TRAILS page 50

Star trails in the north will form a circular path. The circumpolar constellations appear to circle around the North Pole.

Star trails are caused by the earth's movement. Stars do move. Some move only two miles per second. Others travel over five hundred miles per second. However, stars are so far away this movement is not visible and could not be recorded on your film.

EXPERIMENTING WITH BALLOON ROCKETS page 56

Most rockets have a cylindrical airframe which is streamlined to cut through the atmosphere with the least amount of friction. The engines in rockets use a liquid or solid fuel to provide the thrust. In your balloon rockets a gas was used to move it forward and up.

The speed a rocket must go to escape earth's gravity depends upon the payload it is carrying. It must travel over 25,000 mph to head for the moon.

Chapter 3

CAUSING DEW AND FROST TO FORM page 61

Warm air can hold more water vapor than cool air. When the warm air comes in contact with the can of ice the water condenses on the can as the air is cooled. When the temperature of the air and the dew point reading get closer together the relative humidity increases.

MAKING WATER BOIL BY COOLING page 61

When cold water is poured on a capped bottle of very hot water the air pressure in the bottle is reduced. This reduction of pressure permits the air in the water to be released and bubble out. The water is boiling. At high altitudes where the air pressure is less than at sea level the water will boil at a lower temperature. It may take one twice as long to cook potatoes up in a mountain than down in the valley.

Appendix

MAKING A RAINBOW page 62

The brighter spectrum forms the inner bow. Violet light appears on the inside and red light on the outside. The outer rainbow is fainter and the spectrum is reversed.

DISCOVERING FACTORS THAT AFFECT THE FREEZING POINT OF LIQUIDS page 62

Heat is necessary for salt crystals to go into solution. The heat is pulled from the can of milk. This speeds up the freezing time of milk.

Removing the cap from the jar of colored water that is about to freeze will reduce the pressure. Increased pressure produces heat. Releasing the pressure removes the heat and permits the colored water to freeze.

COMPARING TEMPERATURES OF WET AND DRY AIR page 66

The thermometer reading taken in front of a wet towel blowing in the wind should be lower than to the side of the towel where the air is drier. It may be compared to a sling psychrometer. Water molecules hit the bulb of the thermometer and as they evaporate in the moving air heat is necessary. This heat is removed from the thermometer causing a drop in temperature.

EXPERIMENTING WITH CONDENSATION page 66

Condensation is the process of changing a gas to a liquid state. When air is cooled it cannot hold as much moisture and releases it in the form of droplets. The higher the humidity the greater the amount of condensation. If a humidifier is set too high in your house during the winter the water will collect on the inside of the windows. If the temperature outside is real low the condensation will turn to frost.

PRODUCING CONVECTIONS IN AIR page 68

The air above and around the burning candle is being heated. Molecules are moving fast and the space between them is increasing. Hot air is lighter and has less pressure than cold air. Hot air does not rise, however, unless something pushes it. Cooler air under the other chimney will provide this force. As it moves over and pushes the hot air up and out the first chimney, air and smoke above the second chimney move in and down to take its place. A convection current carries heat from one place to another.

Appendix

MAKING FOG   page 68

As the warm moist air expands it hits the cool air coming down from the ice. The molecules of water come together to form minute droplets. This is fog. Eventually these small droplets would form large drops and fall as rain.

A natural fog forms as cool air moves over the ground which has held the heat from the daytime. When the sun comes out the next day a fog is soon "burned off." The droplets of water are broken back up into invisible molecules of water vapor.

MAKING A CLOUD   page 69

Air temperature rises as air is compressed. Warm air holds more moisture than cold air. When air is allowed to expand it cools and will not hold as much moisture. Droplets thus form a cloud. Condensation takes place on the chalk dust in this experiment.

MEASURING HEAT ABSORPTION   page 69

One will find that dark colored paper, such as black, brown, and navy blue, will absorb more heat from the sun's rays than white, yellow, or orange. As heat is absorbed the snow under the paper will melt. The readings on the rulers should prove this.

EXPERIMENTING WITH AIR   page 70

Water forces the air inside the inverted floating bottle to become compressed. The volume of water displaced by the bottle is decreased. The bouyant forced is decreased.

The water in the glass is displaced by air.

The paper does not get wet since the air will not permit water to reach it.

The burning paper on the inside of the jar has burned up the oxygen and the heat has expanded the distance between the molecules in the air. This reduces the air pressure on the inside. Air pressure on the outside or upper end of the egg is greater. This pushes the egg through the neck of the bottle. To get the egg out requires an increase of pressure on the inside. Hold the bottle upside-down at a 45 degree angle with the small end of the egg near the opening. Blow vigorously into the bottle to increase the air pressure. Quickly straighten the bottle to an upside-down position permitting the egg to close off the opening of the bottle. If you have increased air pressure inside the bottle the egg will be pushed out the mouth.

The cardboard should stay on the

Appendix

bottom of the inverted glass of water. At sea level air pressure is 14.7 pounds per square inch. Air pushing on the bottom of the cardboard is greater than the weight of the column of water in the glass. Weigh the water and compare it to the amount of air pressure on the cardboard.

Measure the surface of the newspaper on top of the yardstick. Multiply it times 14.7 pounds per square inch. This is the amount of force holding down the yardstick. If the stick broke when you struck it then the force you used was less than the air holding it down.

The boiling water in the can heated the air. The air expanded, forcing much of it to escape out the opening. When the cap was put on and the air inside began to cool it took up less space. The air pressure on the outside of the can is 14.7 pounds per square inch at sea level. This outside force caused the can to collapse with a pop, crackle, and bang.

WORKING WITH THERMOMETERS   page 74

Everyone knows it is cooler under the shade of an old apple tree than out in a sunny meadow. Usually the surface of sand and water is closer to the air temperature. Deep in the soil and at the bottom of the lake the temperature is lower. Snow acts as a cover and the temperature under a snowbank often is higher than on the surface. Rodents will make tunnels under the snow, scurrying around eating and living as if they were Eskimos in an igloo.

In the second experiment you will find that black absorbs more light and heat than white.

In the last experiment as the temperature falls the liquid will rise in the plastic tube. The air in the top bottle expands when heated. It escapes out the end of the tube into the water and up to the top of the lower bottle. When the air in the upper bottle is cooled it takes up less space so the water rises in the tube.

DISCOVERING FACTORS RELATED TO EVAPORATION   page 76

Sand grains are larger than the other soils and water will run through fast. Packed clay soil has such fine particles the water has difficulty getting through at all. The loam, a combination of sand, clay, silt, and humus, is the best for gardening.

Heat, a greater exposed area, and wind will all increase the rate of evaporation.

Classifying Rocks

STREAK AND HARDNESS CHART
FOR IDENTIFYING ROCKS AND MINERALS

MINERAL	COLOR	STREAK	HARDNESS
Albite (feldspar)	white, bluish, grayish	uncolored	6-6½
Almandite (garnet)	red, purplish-red	white	6½-7½
Analcite	colorless, white	white	5-5½
Apatite	Sea-green, bluish-green, yellow, purple, white	white	5
Arsenopyrite	silver-white to steel gray	grayish black	5½-6
Azurite	azure blue	lighter blue	3½-4
Barite	white, gray, red, blue	white	2½-3½
Beryl	emerald green, light blue, rose-red, blue-green	white	7½-8
Biotite	green to black	uncolored	2½-3
Calcite	white, gray, red, green, blue, violet	white or grayish	3
Celestite	white, pale blue, reddish	white	3-3½
Calcopyrite	brass yellow	greenish-black	3½-4
Cinnabar	cochineal red, dark red	scarlet	2-2½
Copper	copper-red	copper-red	2½-3
Corundum	blue, red, yellow, brown	uncolored	9
Cuprite	red, various shades	brownish-red	3½-4
Diamond	colorless, blue, pink	uncolored	10
Diopside	green, various, dull	white to gray	5-6
Dolomite	white, reddish, brown	white	3½-4
Feldspar (albite)	white, bluish, grayish	uncolored	6
Fluorite	white, green, yellow, blue, violet, red	white	4
Galena	lead-gray	lead-gray	2½
Gold	gold yellow to pale yellow	yellow	2½-3
Graphite	iron-black to dark steel-gray	steel-gray	1-2
Gypsum	usually white	white	1½-2
Halite	colorless or white	white	5½-6½
Hematite	steel gray, red, brown	reddish-brown	5½-6½
Hornblende	dark green to black	uncolored	
		very pale	5-6
Kyanite	blue, white, green	uncolored	5-7½
Limonite	brown	yellowish-brown	5-5½
Magnetite	iron-black	black	5½-6½
Malachite	bright green	paler green	3½-4
Molybdenite	pure-lead gray	greenish-gray	1-1½
Muscovite	colorless, brown, pale green	uncolored	2-2½
Natrolite	white, colorless	uncolored	5-5½
Opal	white, yellow, red, brown, green, sometimes rich play of colors	white	5½-6½
Pectolite	whitish or grayish	white	5

MINERAL	COLOR	STREAK	HARDNESS
Pyrite	pale brass-yellow	greenish-black	6-6½
Quartz			
Rock crystal	colorless	uncolored	7
Amethyst	purple	uncolored	7
Smoky	smoky, black	uncolored	7
Rose	pink	uncolored	7
Agate	several colors, banded	uncolored	7
Jasper	red, brown, green	uncolored	7
Chalcedony	tan, white, blue	uncolored	7
Flint	gray, brown, black	uncolored	7
Rhodonite	brownish-red, flesh red, rose-pink	white	5½-6½
Serpentine	leek-green, brownish yellow	white	2½-4
Siderite	ash-gray, brown, brownish-red	white	3½-4
Silver	silver-white	silver-white	2½-3
Sphalerite	yellow, brown, black	brownish to light yellow	3½-4
Spinel	red, blue, green, black	white	8
Staurolite	dark reddish-brown	uncolored	7-7½
Stilbite	white, brown	uncolored	3½-4
Sulfur	sulfur-yellow, honey-yellow	white	1½-2½
Talc	apple-green to white	usually white	1-1½
Topaz	straw-yellow, blue, white, colorless	uncolored	8
Tourmaline	black, blue, green, red, yellow, often several zones of color	uncolored	7-7½
Tremolite	white, gray, green	uncolored	5-6
Uraninite	velvet-black, greenish	brownish-black	5½
Zircon	brown, green, blue, colorless	uncolored	7½

Index

Index

Index

Helen J. Challand earned her M.A. and Ph.D. from Northwestern University. She currently is Chair of the Science Department at National College of Education and Coordinator of Undergraduate Studies for the college's West Suburban Campus.

An experienced classroom teacher and science consultant, Dr. Challand has worked on science projects for Scott Foresman and Company, Rand McNally Publishers, Harper-Row Publishers, Encyclopedia Britannica Films, Coronet Films, and Journal Films. She is associate editor for the *Young People's Science Encyclopedia* published by Childrens Press.